catching
readers

4/5

THE RESEARCH-INFORMED CLASSROOM SERIES

Consider daily life for a child struggling with reading. Imagine what it is like to go through school day after day feeling that you are bad at the one thing that school seems to value most. Imagine struggling with everything from independent reading to reading directions on a math worksheet. Imagine what that feels like . . . .

While there are all sorts of pressures to improve instruction for struggling readers—to raise test scores, to make adequate yearly progress (AYP), and so on—the most compelling reason is to help as many children as possible avoid that feeling. We want to enable children to go through elementary school feeling, and being, successful.

Barbara Taylor brings decades of research and development to the question of how to help struggling readers become successful. *Catching Readers: Grades 4/5*, which is part of the Early Intervention in Reading series, brings the resulting insights to you, in the form of concrete and specific practices that have been shown to help children who struggle improve their reading. These books could not come at a more important time, as response to intervention (RTI) leads schools to invest more than ever in small-group reading instruction. The multifaceted and responsive teaching at the heart of the approach Taylor describes is a welcome contrast to the myopic, scripted programs marketed so heavily under the banner of RTI.

These books exemplify the ideals of the Research-Informed Classroom series—bringing rigorous classroom-based research to bear on persistent challenges of classroom practice. This series aims to bridge the gap between research and practice by focusing on the most practical, classroom-relevant research and communicating practices based on that research in a way that makes them accessible, appealing, and actionable. The series is founded on the belief that students and teachers are researchers' clients, and serving them should be the highest priority.

As with so much of the best educational research and development, Taylor has collaborated extensively with teachers close to home and throughout the United States. Indeed, one might say we've gone full circle, from Teacher-Informed Research to Research-Informed Teaching. So thank you, teachers, and thank you, Barbara, for this important contribution to reading success for all children.

— *Nell K. Duke*
MICHIGAN STATE UNIVERSITY

catching readers

grades **4/5**

DAY-BY-DAY SMALL-GROUP READING INTERVENTIONS

Barbara M. Taylor

HEINEMANN
Portsmouth, NH

KH

Heinemann
361 Hanover Street
Portsmouth, NH 03801–3912
www.heinemann.com

Offices and agents throughout the world

The author and publisher wish to thank those who have generously given permission to reprint borrowed material in this book and/or on the DVD:

Cover image and excerpt from *Germs Make Me Sick* by Melvin Berger, illustrations by Marilyn Hafner. Text copyright © 1985, 1995 by Melvin Berger. Illustrations copyright © 1995 by Marilyn Hafner. Published by HarperCollins Publishers. Reproduced by permission of the publisher.

Library of Congress Cataloging-in-Publication Data
Taylor, Barbara M.
   Catching readers, grades 4/5 : day-by-day small-group reading interventions / Barbara M. Taylor.
      p. cm.—(Early intervention in reading series) (The research-informed classroom series)
   Includes bibliographical references.
   ISBN-13: 978-0-325-02891-0
   ISBN-10: 0-325-02891-5
   1. Reading—Remedial teaching. 2. Reading (Elementary).
3. Individualized instruction. I. Title.
   LB1050.5.T336 2011
   372.41'62—dc22   2010049851

Editor: Margaret LaRaia
Production editor: Patricia Adams
Video editor: Sherry Day
Video producer: Bob Schuster, Real Productions
Cover design: Lisa Fowler
Typesetter: Eric Rosenbloom, Kirby Mountain Composition
Manufacturing: Valerie Cooper and Steve Bernier

Printed in the United States of America on acid-free paper

15 14 13 12 11   ML   1 2 3 4 5

3/15/13

This book is dedicated to the many fourth- and fifth-grade teachers who work tirelessly to provide motivating instruction that meets their students' needs, challenges them all, and is instrumental to their success in reading.

Contents

Helping Fourth and Fifth Graders Who Struggle
Lessons That Sit Within Effective Reading Instruction   **1**

Meet the Teachers
The Differentiated Lessons and Teacher Collaboration That Support EIR   **15**

Managing Your Reading Block with EIR 85

Creating an EIR Community 99

On the DVD

video

See-It-in-Action Video Clips

Video 1 Activate Prior Knowledge

Video 2 Decode and Discuss Words

Video 3 Coach for Comprehension

Video 4 Review Reciprocal Teaching

Video 5 Practice Reciprocal Teaching

Video 6 Prepare for Partner Reading

Video 7 Review Buddy Reading Strategies

Video 8 Partner Reading

Video 9 Discuss Tutoring

Video 10 Other Uses for Reciprocal Teaching

 Downloadable Classroom Reproducibles

More than 100 pages of full-size forms and teaching resources.

Teaching Resources on the DVD

Chapter 5

Chapter 6

Chapter 7

Foreword

I began my teaching career as a first-grade teacher in Key West, Florida, in 1965. Much has changed since then in the world and in the world of school. But reading Barbara Taylor's books made me realize how much is still the same. My class of thirty-five children contained nine children—two girls and seven boys—who were (in the lingo of the day) "not ready." In those days, basal reading series for first grade had a readiness book that I was very grateful to find. I grouped these nine students together and we made our way through the workbook pages. The pages were mostly practice with letter names and auditory discrimination—the precursor of phonemic awareness. Six weeks into the school year, we finished the readiness book and I administered the Metropolitan Readiness Test to my students. For three days, I tried to keep them focused on the correct lines and asked them to underline the letter *b*, put an *x* on the picture that began like *paint*, and circle the picture of the object that rhymed with *cat*. I took all these booklets home and spent a miserable weekend grading them. As I made my way through the test booklets, I adopted a "benefit of the doubt" scoring system. "Two red marks on this line, none on the next. If the second mark is on the next line, it would be right. I'm counting it correct." In spite of my lenient scoring, scores for eight of the nine children indicated they were still "not ready." I spent a sleepless Sunday night wondering what I was to do with these children who were clearly not ready when I had used up all the readiness materials! Lacking any alternative, I started them in the first pre-primer and we plodded our way through the books. By the end of the year, only one of these students could read fluently at primer level.

If Barbara had written her books 45 years earlier (when she was probably in kindergarten), I think I could have transformed my "not ready" kids into fluent readers. Based on many years of research in real classrooms with real teachers and kids, Barbara has created a workable system for providing struggling readers in grades K–5 with the targeted intervention they need to become fluent readers. At the heart of Early Intervention in Reading (EIR) is the addition of a second reading lesson in a small-group setting. Unlike many interventions, struggling readers get this second reading lesson *in addition to* all the rich classroom instruction and *in* the classroom—not in some room down the hall. With details, specifics, and examples that only someone who has spent many hours in the classroom could know, Barbara guides you step-by-step as you organize for and provide effective EIR instruction. As you read through the book, your brain races with questions:

▶ "How do I fit an additional intervention group lesson into my daily schedule?"

▶ "What books work best for these lessons?"

▶ "How can I provide all the instruction struggling readers need in 20 minutes?"

▶ "What does the coaching for decoding and comprehension look like and sound like?"

▶ "How do I wean them off my coaching and move them toward independence?"

▶ "How do I provide worthwhile independent activities for the students I am not working with?"

Because Barbara has worked in so many classrooms coaching teachers who are implementing EIR, she can provide practical, classroom-tested answers to all your questions. She invites you into the classrooms of real teachers and you get to hear them describing how they organize and problem solve. In addition to the printed resource, you can go to the video clips on the DVD to "See It in Action." As you watch real teachers move through the three-day lesson sequence, you realize that, while it is complex, Barbara provides all the resources you need to make it work in your classrooms with your students who struggle.

Once you see how EIR works in your classroom, you will probably want to spread the word. Not to worry! Barbara is right there supporting you. In the final chapter, "Creating an EIR Community," she provides a detailed, month-by-month plan for organizing a group of colleagues to learn together how to better meet the needs of struggling readers.

So, if they ever invent a time machine that could transport me back to 1965, with the help of Barbara Taylor's books, I know I could teach all my "not ready" kids to read!

Patricia M. Cunningham
Wake Forest University

Acknowledgments

• •

This book is the result of fifteen years of collaboration with many fourth- and fifth-grade teachers and colleagues across the United States. I want to thank them all for their invaluable contributions to this book.

Inspired by Reading Recovery, I developed the Early Intervention in Reading (EIR) process in the late 1980s to help first-grade teachers help their at-risk readers succeed in reading through daily, small-group, reading intervention lessons. I have refined the EIR process over the years by visiting many classrooms and learning from many teachers and their students. Without this opportunity, I would not have been able to modify and improve the EIR teaching strategies and professional learning practices described in this book.

I also want to thank the hundreds of fourth- and fifth-grade teachers I have visited and learned from over the past ten years through my work on effective reading instruction and schoolwide reading improvement. I especially want to thank the exemplary teachers who have contributed so much to the book by sharing their thoughts and lessons related to effective reading instruction.

I owe a special thanks and a debt of gratitude to my colleague, Ceil Critchely, a master teacher who has been instrumental in helping teachers succeed with EIR through the phenomenal professional learning support she has provided to them over the past twelve years. I know that without Ceil's expert guidance, teachers would not have been as successful as they have been in helping their at-risk readers learn to read well by the end of third grade.

I also want to thank my academic colleagues for their support and feedback. In particular, I want to recognize my good friends, Kathy Au and Taffy Raphael, who have gently nudged me over the years to publish my work on EIR in a form readily accessible to teachers.

I want to thank the many people at Heinemann who have made this book possible. I especially want to thank Patty Adams, my production editor, for her top-notch work on a complex project within a challenging time frame. Whenever I called with questions or concerns, she responded cheerfully and promptly. Many others at Heinemann have also contributed to this book and I thank them for their efforts.

It is my sincere hope that fourth- and fifth-grade teachers will find this book useful as they strive to teach students who come to them a little behind in the fall to be confident, successful, readers by the end of the school year. Thanks to all fourth- and fifth-grade teachers reading this book for the important work you do for our children!

Barbara M. Taylor
University of Minnesota

Introduction

● ●

We are a culture of quick fixes. We promise mastery in ten easy lessons, instant success, overnight sensations. Go to a bookstore and whether you stand and gaze at the brightly colored covers in the business, health, or education section, the answer to our every need is couched in words like *speedy*, *easy*, and *seven easy steps*.

In such a culture, a lot of alarm bells go off when a teacher faces a nine-year-old child in fourth grade who is behind in learning to read. *Catching Readers, Grades 4/5*, is one book in a series of five, dedicated to giving the regular classroom teacher what's needed to reach and teach that nine-year-old with a concrete plan rather than a frantic pull-out program or a misguided label. Each book in the series offers teacher-friendly, research-proven background and lessons for young readers who need an extra boost.

The intervention model brings reading success to children in a five-day lesson cycle, which I know sounds as though I'm playing into the same glib promises of swift solutions. I state it here as a way to express that it is a five-day format used across a school year with deep roots—more than fifteen years of classroom testing. I emphasize the "five-day" repetition of the lessons to make it clear that we don't have to choose to run around in circles looking for some new complicated program for reaching at-risk readers. We know what to do. When we're true to children's developmental levels, know which books to put in their hands, and provide effective instruction, a lot of good things fall into place. The key is to focus on the children and the practices we know help them to read at each grade level.

In fact, the intervention model I offer stands in opposition to approaches and programs that think the answer to helping K–5 below-grade-level readers achieve is to provide remediation. Above-grade-level, on-grade-level, and below-grade-level readers all need the same thing: sound teaching techniques and developmentally appropriate practices that meet their needs and provide intellectual challenge to all.

Here's an overview of how the interventions are unique and yet similar for each grade level, so you can see the developmentally based, purposeful overlap in the series. The intervention gives teachers, staff developers, principals, and reading coaches a predictable model so that schoolwide coherence is easier to attain. All grade-level models stress word-recognition proficiency, high-level comprehension, vocabulary development, and strategic reading. Unique components of the various grade-specific models are described below:

Kindergarten

The daily 10-minute supplemental lessons for kindergarten focus on developing all children's oral language, phonemic awareness, and emergent literacy abilities through literature-based activities. The goal is for all students to leave kindergarten with the skills they need to learn to read in first grade. The more capable children, as they respond to the various activities in EIR lessons, serve as models for the children who are less skilled in oral language and emergent literacy abilities. Less-skilled children who need more support return to some of the story discussion questions and phonemic awareness/emergent literacy activities for an additional 10 minutes a day.

First Grade

First-grade children who start the school year with lower-than-average phonemic awareness abilities and letter-sound knowledge will benefit from EIR lessons. The teacher focuses on accelerating students' literacy learning by deliberately coaching them to use strategies to decode words as they read, to actively engage in word work, and to think at a higher level about the meaning of the texts they are reading.

Second Grade

Second-grade readers who can't read a book at a first-grade level at the start of second grade will benefit from the basic EIR routine. The intervention begins with first-grade books and routines of the grade 1 EIR model and then moves into second-grade books a few months later. There is also an accelerated grade 2 routine designed for students who come to second grade as independent readers but who will need additional support to be reading on grade level by the end of the school year.

Third Grade

The grade 3 EIR routine is for children who are reading below grade level when they enter third grade. In the grade 3 EIR model, the focus is on refining students' decoding of multisyllabic words, improving their fluency, developing their vocabulary, and enhancing their comprehension of narrative and informational texts. Ideally, the grade 3 EIR model is done within the context of a cross-age tutoring program in which the third-grade students read to and also tutor first-grade EIR students. The third graders are working on their reading for more than "catching up because they are behind." They look forward to and enjoy working with their younger students who needs additional support in reading.

Fourth/Fifth Grade

The EIR routine for fourth and fifth grade is for children who are reading below grade level at the beginning of the school year. Although students receive support in attacking multisyllabic words and developing reading fluency, the grade 4/5 model focuses on improving students' comprehension of informational text through the use of comprehension strategies, discussion of vocabulary, and engagement in high-level talk and writing about texts. Ideally, the grade 4/5 EIR model is done within the context of a motivating cross-age tutoring program in which fourth and fifth graders read to and also tutor second or third graders.

Getting Good at It: Different Ways to Use This Book

This book—and by extension all the books in this series—is designed to be used by the individual teacher, a pair or group of teachers, or as part of a schoolwide professional development plan. Here are components that support collaborative learning:

Video Clips for Individual Viewing

As you read about the recurring cycle of EIR routines, I encourage you to watch the video clips that illustrate what is being covered in the text. Many teachers have told me that seeing the EIR routines being applied in the classroom makes it easy to start teaching the EIR lessons. See this icon throughout the book for easy access to the video clips and teaching resources on the DVD.

Guidance for Monthly Sessions with Colleagues

In the last chapter, "Creating an EIR Community," I share a model for a professional learning community (PLC) that works. Over my many years of working with teachers on effective reading instruction generally, and EIR lessons specifically, I have learned from teachers' comments that the collaborative nature of learning new instructional techniques with colleagues leads to excellent understanding, reflection, and success.

Website Support

For additional support, go to www.Heinemann.com and search by Taylor or *Catching Readers* for answers to questions that will likely arise about teaching EIR lessons. Also, go to www.earlyinterventioninreading.com to learn more about the availability of additional support from an EIR expert.

We can help so many children become successful readers when we offer excellent reading instruction and provide effective interventions to those students who require additional reading support within their classroom setting. I am excited to have the opportunity to offer my *Catching Readers* series of books to you. Thank you for the important work you do for our children!

catching
readers

Helping Fourth and Fifth Graders Who Struggle

Lessons That Sit Within Effective Reading Instruction

Fourth and fifth graders are growing rapidly. As preteens, they are very social; in their interactions with peers, appearances increasingly matter to them and they are self-conscious at times. They remain curious and excited about learning, however, and they like to collaborate with other students when given the opportunity. In general, students in fourth and fifth grade read fluently, but many of those who struggle with reading typically do so because of difficulties with comprehension.

Catching Readers, Grades 4/5 is designed to help you meet the needs of your students who are reading one to two years below grade level. Although the book's focus is primarily on improving students' reading comprehension abilities through comprehension strategy instruction, high-level talk and writing about text, and vocabulary development, word-recognition accuracy and fluency are also dealt with as needed. You'll also learn about effective differentiated reading instruction for all students.

My career as a researcher and teacher educator has been dedicated to studying and describing components of effective literacy instruction so that teachers can become more intentional in their teaching and more confident in their interactions with children around all aspects of reading instruction, including whole-class and small-group reading lessons, word recognition, vocabulary, comprehension instruction, and more. And so this intervention model—Early Intervention in Reading (EIR®)—doesn't stand separate from but sits within the regular classroom literacy instruction. To illustrate how this model works, I highlight the work of three outstanding fourth- and fifth-grade teachers who use EIR within their literacy block in Chapter 2. They find their students' reading abilities grow tremendously during the year. These teachers share their ideas about differentiated instruction to meet individual needs and the operation of an effective literacy block, during which children engage in lots of authentic reading, writing, and talk.

How the Early Intervention in Reading Model Sits Within Effective Reading Instruction

The small-group intervention lessons featured in this book are based on EIR, which is a set of teaching practices I developed that incorporates the characteristics of effective reading instruction (see page 3). The fourth- and fifth-grade program has been in practice for more than fifteen years in schools, and if you're a teacher looking to implement response to intervention (RTI) or differentiated instruction, you'll see that my model can easily be viewed—and used—to meet these current calls to action. Early Intervention in Reading provides:

▶ fourth and fifth graders who are reading below grade level an additional daily opportunity to interact with text in a structured, consistent, and comfortable small-group setting

▶ fourth- and fifth-grade teachers a framework that will show them how to support these children so they can catch up or keep up with grade-level expectations for reading

▶ teachers and schools an intervention model that isn't stigmatizing for children because it uses authentic literature and practices, and takes place within the regular classroom—and usually by the classroom teacher; it ideally includes cross-age tutoring in which students work with younger children who need extra reading support

Through structured, 20-minute lessons, a group of struggling readers are provided with an extra shot of daily quality reading instruction. Teachers support and coach individual students based on need, thus accelerating students'

How EIR Meets the Requirements of Effective Reading Instruction

	Effective Reading Instruction	EIR Lessons
What You Teach (Content)	Word-recognition instruction	Decoding multisyllabic words, coaching in word-recognition strategies
	Rereading for fluency	Repeated reading of texts, coached reading with feedback
	Text-based vocabulary instruction	Discussion of word meanings at point of contact in EIR stories
	Comprehension strategies instruction	Summarizing stories, practicing comprehension monitoring, generating and answering questions that require high-level thinking
	Comprehension instruction in the context of high-level talk about text	Coaching for comprehension and high-level talk about text
How You Teach (Pedagogy)	Application of taught skills and strategies to text	Much of the EIR lesson involves applying taught skills and strategies to text
	Differentiated instruction	EIR lessons are an extra shot of quality instruction for struggling readers in which the teacher provides support to individual students based on need
	Balance direct teaching with providing support	After teaching skills and strategies, the teacher spends much of the EIR lesson coaching them to use these skills and strategies as they read EIR texts
	Teaching with clear purpose and good timing	Teacher states lesson purposes routinely, teaches daily steps of each 20-minute EIR lesson at a rapid pace
	Active student engagement	All students read, write, talk, and share in the small group or with a partner
	Student engagement in challenging, motivating learning activities	Students read engaging texts that they will then discuss with grade 2 or 3 EIR reading buddies who are also in EIR groups. Fifth graders coach their younger reading buddies with their EIR stories as well.
	Developing independent learners	High expectations, releasing to students, responsibility, partner work, developing students' self-confidence through tutoring of younger readers who are experiencing difficulties in learning to read
	Motivating classroom community	Using praise, helpful feedback, demonstrating enthusiasm for learning
Professional Learning	Collaborative learning with a focus on practice	Monthly learning meetings to discuss EIR strategies, successes, and challenges

reading progress. We'll look at the basic components of the EIR routines, and in Chapter 3 we will review the five-day lesson cycle in detail, but here's a quick glimpse of how these lessons amplify the effective reading instruction.

Which Children Need the Intervention and What Is the End Goal?

Students who benefit from this intervention are those who enter grades 4/5 reading one or two years below grade level. The lessons focus on building students' reading fluency and comprehension. Ideally, the model uses a cross-age tutoring component in which students work for three days on an informational book that they will then read on the fourth day to a second- or third-grade student who is also reading below grade level.

Children who fall below 90 percent accuracy on a third- or fourth-grade passage (e.g., one that is a grade level below their grade placement) typically need supplemental help in word recognition. Fourth graders who read less than 75 words correctly per minute (wcpm) and fifth graders who read less than 90 wcpm on an informal reading inventory most likely need to work on fluency. Children who can tell little about a third- or fourth-grade informal reading inventory passage (e.g., they get a score of 1 or 2 on the summarizing rubric discussed in Chapter 5 on a passage one grade level below their grade placement) or are at the frustration level (lower than 70 percent correct) on informal reading inventory questions may need to work on comprehension. In Chapter 5, I describe assessments you can use to determine which students might benefit from EIR.

Scores on informal reading inventories administered to seventy-one fourth graders (in four schools) who were reading a year or more below grade level in the fall and received EIR lessons during the year revealed that 98 percent were able to decode fourth-grade-level passages with at least 92 percent word-recognition accuracy in May (Taylor 2001). Although their fluency was still slightly below average, their mean fluency score went from 77 to 108 wcpm from the beginning to the end of the school year.

All twenty-six fifth graders (in two schools) who were reading a year or more below grade level in the fall and received EIR lessons during the year were able to decode fifth-grade-level passages with at least 92 percent word-recognition accuracy on an informal reading inventory administered in May. Although their fluency was still slightly below average, their mean fluency score went from 82 to 109 wcpm from the beginning to the end of the school year.

Teachers report that the children in the grades 4/5 EIR program take their tutoring very seriously and enjoy it immensely. In addition to improving students' reading ability, I have found that the cross-age tutoring component of the EIR program enhances students' attitudes and self-concepts as readers (Taylor et al. 1997).

The What and How of Good Fourth- and Fifth-Grade Teaching

EIR was developed with key elements of content (the what) and pedagogy (the how) as its foundation. Effective teachers tend to have a great day-to-day awareness of both content and pedagogy. With that in mind, in Chapter 2 you will meet three teachers, Katie Tanner, Eric Brown, and Maria Martinez, and see what effective teaching looks like in urban, suburban, and rural settings. You'll gain a sense of how these teachers connect EIR lessons to their overall reading instruction. These three teachers not only teach EIR lessons but also provide effective reading instruction to all their students and see excellent growth in their students' reading abilities during each school year.

Content: Four Dimensions Elementary Students Need

The content of effective reading instruction has the following dimensions, all of which develop students' abilities to become competent readers. These dimensions have a sound body of reading research behind them, as will be noted in the sections that follow:

- word-recognition development

- fluency development

- vocabulary development

- comprehension development

Does this list comprise a complete universe of what leads children to become successful, engaged readers? No, but these dimensions are the nonnegotiable aspects of teaching reading. Without them, all the other practices don't have a sufficient foundation.

Word-Recognition Development

Most students in kindergarten and first grade and many in second grade benefit from systematic, explicit instruction in phonemic awareness and phonics (Adams 1990; National Reading Panel [NRP] 2000; Snow et al. 1998). Typically, by third grade most students, even those who are reading below grade level, know their symbol-sound correspondences. However, many third, fourth, and fifth graders who are not yet reading on a third-grade level benefit from phonics instruction that focuses on how to decode multisyllabic words. Coaching students to use word-recognition strategies as they read texts is another important aspect of decoding instruction for below-grade-level readers in fourth and fifth grade. For example, when students in Maria's EIR group get stuck on the word *orangutan* (one student has not looked carefully at the entire word and calls it *orange tang*), Maria coaches students to break the word into chunks. They come up with *or-ang-u-tan*. They have to be flexible with the /u/ sound in the word, trying *oo*, as in *rule*, after first trying the short *u*, but do come up with the correct schwa pronunciation and go on to discuss the word.

Fluency Development

Developing *fluency*, or reading at a good rate with appropriate phrasing, is important since fluent reading supports comprehension. Oral reading procedures to develop fluency, in which students receive guidance or support, can have a significant impact on the reading abilities of below-grade-level readers (Kuhn and Stahl 2003). Procedures to build fluency include repeated reading and coached reading, as well as ample opportunities for students to read books at their independent and instructional reading levels. Effective reading instruction weaves fluency practice into whole-group and small-group lessons, as well as independent work activities.

Vocabulary Development

When it comes to developing students' vocabulary, a variety of approaches is critical. The approaches (Baumann and Kame'enui 2004; Blachowicz and Fisher 2000; Graves 2007) include:

▶ direct instruction in specific words

▶ prereading instruction in words

▶ learning to use strategies to determine word meanings

▶ learning of words in rich contexts and incidentally through wide reading

▶ studying words that children will find useful in many contexts (Beck et al. 2002)

Three points are worth emphasizing. First, some words need to be introduced before reading so that students are not confused about major aspects of a story. Second, teachers sometimes do insufficient vocabulary instruction *during* and *after* the reading of a story. Beck and colleagues (2002) stress the value of teaching many word meanings at point of contact in the text. When Eric Brown has students read in groups of three about desert animals, he instructs them to look for "million dollar words" that describe the animals. Later in a whole-group meeting students will share the words they found and what they mean. Third, developing students' curiosity about words is also important. You can model this interest in word meanings and enthusiasm for authors' word choice in a variety of ways, and it's a boon to students' reading and writing. For example, Eric Brown talks with great enthusiasm about the words that describe desert animals that students will find and share.

Comprehension Development

Skilled readers use strategies to enhance their comprehension. Also, research has shown that explicit instruction in comprehension strategies improves stu-

dents' reading comprehension abilities (Foorman et al. 2006; Guthrie et al. 2000; National Reading Panel 2000). Explicit lessons are most effective in the following strategies: summarizing; monitoring comprehension; using graphic and semantic organizers before, during, and after reading; using story structure; answering questions; and generating questions (NRP 2000). Also, teaching students to use multiple comprehension strategies, such as with reciprocal teaching, in naturalistic contexts is important to students' growth in reading comprehension abilities (Guthrie et al. 2004; Klingner et al. 2004; National Reading Panel 2000; Pressley 2006). The classroom example in Chapter 2 of Eric Brown exemplifies instruction in summarizing informational text and using multiple comprehension strategies.

Teaching students how to engage in high-level talk and writing about text is another vital aspect of comprehension instruction repeatedly found to be related to reading gains (Knapp 1995; McKeown et al. 2009; Saunders and Goldenberg 1999; Taylor et al. 2003; Van den Branden 2000; Wilkinson 2009). For example, in Chapter 2, we read about Katie Tanner and her students discussing the character traits and actions of Melly and Anny Beth (the two main characters in *Turnabout* [Haddix 2000], who have taken an injection that makes them grow younger every year. After the discussion, students are asked to write about whether they would have taken the injection to get younger and then defend their position.

Pedagogy: The Art of Teaching Demystified

You know good teaching when you see it, and yet it can be hard to capture all the nuances of it in the confines of a book. In short, good teaching consists of all the teacher's routines and practices, as well as his or her ability to respond in the moment to students' needs and to connect to students so they feel motivated to learn. For example, techniques like clearly stating lesson purposes or offering impromptu coaching, as well as decisions that need to be made about things such as timing (e.g., how long to spend on a particular aspect of a lesson) or what texts and tasks to use to engage students in purposeful learning activities, are part of the pedagogy of teaching.

Affective Dimensions: What It Means to Be Motivating to Kids

Another important aspect of pedagogy includes the "people skills" involved in teaching. Research and our own experiences have a lot to tell us about the impact of teachers' management, expectations, and attitudes toward learning on children's achievement and motivation. As you read the characteristics listed in the boxes that follow, think about your fourth- or fifth-grade students and how you view yourself in relation to these aspects of effective teaching.

Elements of Effective Pedagogy

Effective teachers skillfully coordinate many pedagogical aspects of their reading lessons. They make sure that they:

▶ Strike a good balance between whole-group and small-group instruction, using the form that best meets lesson objectives (Chorzempa and Graham 2006; Pressley et al. 1998)

▶ Consider the purposes and timing of their lessons relative to their students' varying instructional needs

▶ Balance direct teaching (telling, leading) with differentiated support (e.g., coaching, providing feedback) as students are engaged in learning activities (Allington and Johnston 2002; Connor et al. 2004; Pressley et al. 2003; Taylor et al. 2003)

▶ Foster students' active involvement in literacy activities to enhance their learning and motivation (Allington and Johnston 2002; Guthrie et al. 2000)

▶ Provide students with challenging, motivating activities as they are working with the teacher, on their own, or with other students (Allington and Johnston 2002; Pressley et al. 2003)

▶ Sustain a balanced approach to instruction that involves direct teaching of reading skills and strategies as well as giving students opportunities to apply skills and strategies to engaging texts through reading, writing, and discussing (Allington and Johnston 2002; Pressley 2007)

▶ Provide differentiated instruction and make good choices in the use of instructional materials based on students' abilities and interests (Pressley et al. 2007)

▶ Sustain culturally responsive instruction, which includes building on students' cultural strengths in structuring student interactions and using multicultural literature to celebrate students' cultural heritages and introduce new cultural perspectives (Au 2006)

▶ Continually assess students' engagement, understanding, and behavior throughout the day (Allington and Johnston 2002; Pressley et al. 2003)

▶ Systematically collect and share a variety of formal and informal student assessment data to help them make instructional decisions to improve student performance (Lipson et al. 2004; Taylor et al. 2000). Data might include diagnostic, formative (on-the-go assessment as kids work), and summative assessments (checking to see whether students understand something at the end of learning)

Additional Motivating Pedagogical Practices

Effective teachers in the elementary grades:

▶ Maintain a positive classroom atmosphere and teach with enthusiasm for learning (Allington and Johnston 2002; Dolezal et al. 2003; Pressley et al. 2003)

▶ Expertly manage and organize their classrooms (Allington and Johnston 2002; Dolezal et al. 2003; Pressley 2001, 2006; Taylor, Pressley, and Pearson 2002)

▶ Provide encouragement and praise as well as positive feedback (Pressley et al. 2007)

▶ Have high expectations for their students, communicate to students that effort leads to success, encourage independence and responsibility, provide students with choice, and foster cooperative learning experiences (Allington and Johnston 2002; Bohn et al. 2004; Dolezal et al. 2003; Guthrie et al. 2004; Hamre and Pianta 2005; Pressley et al. 2003)

Collaborate with Colleagues

While individual teachers can positively improve their reading instruction and thus the development of their students' reading, it is often helpful to work with colleagues as you embark on the journey of being the most effective teacher you can be. Katie, Eric, and Maria all believe that collaboration is extremely instrumental to their success. They will share some of their ideas on the value of collaboration in Chapter 2. In Chapter 7, I provide guidance on implementing EIR schoolwide.

Having a good grasp of the content and pedagogy of effective reading instruction will inform your practice and support you in the many decisions you need to make in your day-to-day reading lessons. In turn, effective practices will help your students develop into motivated, competent readers.

A Five-Day Cycle of Supplemental Instruction

Now that we have looked at effective reading instruction for all students, let's turn to an overview of the EIR model for students who need additional support. It is important that children who are not reading on grade level experience success in reading, and EIR is structured so they will. The EIR model works on a five-day cycle. Its predictable structure provides consistency for struggling readers and helps build their confidence. During the five-day cycle of lessons, students are supported through the following practices:

▶ Active engagement

▶ Coaching in decoding multisyllabic words and using word-recognition strategies

▶ Repeated reading for fluency

▶ Comprehension and vocabulary instruction

▶ Guidance and support on their teaching and coaching of younger reading buddies

▶ Regular monitoring progress

Active Engagement

Students are busy participating in reading experiences throughout the 20-minute small-group session. During this time students engage in several activities that address different elements essential to learning to read. This 20-minute session is considered to be acceleration, unlike remediation, and implies that the children receiving this intervention can learn to read before they fall too far behind. In EIR, children typically enjoy the small-group routine and stay actively engaged during the lesson.

Repeated Reading for Fluency

Students read and reread texts. They read informational texts by taking turns, with a partner, and independently, which helps them experience fluent reading as well as the feeling of success. As they reread, their word-recognition accuracy, automaticity, and fluency develop.

Decoding Multisyllabic Words and Coaching in the Use of Multiple Word-Recognition Strategies

Decoding support is given while children read and involves modeling, asking questions, or giving prompts related to words children don't know. This coaching enables children to succeed at figuring out a word they don't instantly recognize while they are reading. Typically, in fourth and fifth grade, children need strategies and coaching support as they gain confidence in decoding multisyllabic words.

The coaching also helps children learn to self-monitor their word-recognition attempts. For example, if a child comes to a word, reads it incorrectly, and then self-corrects it, this is a good example of self-monitoring.

Complimenting children for their attempts (e.g., "Good checking, how did you know to try that word again?") is an integral part of the instruction, because the praise and questions encourage children to be aware of the strategies they are using to make sense of texts. You also want students to notice instances when words they say don't make sense in the context of the story or don't look like the actual word they are trying to read. Part of self-monitoring is learning to cross-check; that is, not only being sure a word looks like the word on the page but also being sure that a word makes sense in the story, or vice versa.

Coaching to Develop Student Independence

An important part of coaching students in word-recognition strategies is releasing responsibility to the children as soon as possible. Typically, at first, you will have to model or demonstrate for them how to use a variety of strategies to figure out words they do not decode correctly and follow up this modeling with coaching as students try to sound out words themselves. Often, however, we inadvertently coach struggling readers too much for too long, and the students don't learn to depend on themselves as readers. As the year progresses, teachers need to use more general prompts (e.g., "What can you do?" Or, "Look at that again. Can you break it into chunks?") and focus on their wait time so that students have enough time to problem-solve and figure out words themselves. When I am coaching children, I feel successful when they come to a hard word in the text and don't look up at me for the answer. It's important to praise them for this independence and remind them that this is what they need to continue to do when they are reading on their own.

Comprehension Instruction and Vocabulary Development

Teaching struggling readers to read for meaning is very important, but it is sometimes neglected because the focus is on teaching students to develop their word-recognition fluency and ability to decode grade-level texts. To send the message that reading for meaning is what reading is all about, teachers in EIR lessons discuss the meaning of potentially unfamiliar words they come across in the text and ask questions about the text that:

- Expand students' comprehension of the text

- Stretch their thinking

- Relate the passage to their lives

- Involve them in summarizing

As students answer thought-provoking questions, the teacher coaches them to elaborate on their ideas. I call this part of the EIR lesson "coaching for comprehension." Students also learn and practice comprehension strategies such as monitoring comprehension, asking and answering questions, summarizing, and predicting.

Reading Block: Katie's Sample Schedule

9:00–9:10   Whole-Group Lesson

- Use a selection from a basal reader or trade book
- Target a comprehension strategy
- Teach vocabulary at point of contact in the selection
- Pose and discuss answers to high-level questions
- Review learning activities for independent work time

9:10–10:05   Independent and Small-Group Work

Independent Work: While the teacher is working with small groups of students, the other students work independently or with a partner or small group on challenging and differentiated materials (see Chapter 6 for a more in-depth discussion of independent work activities). For example, students might:

- Read book club selections as directed by the teacher
- Write in a journal or on open-ended response sheets about what they have read
- Talk with others about what they have read
- Write down new or interesting vocabulary and possible word meanings
- Read/reread for pleasure, fiction and nonfiction books of their own choosing
- Research and write about a topic being covered in social studies or science

Small Group 1 (9:10–9:25)

Using a text at students' reading level, the teacher

- Provides instruction in decoding multisyllablic words, as needed
- Discusses a few word meanings prior to reading, but teaches more vocabulary at point of contact in the text and after reading
- Follows up on the comprehension strategy targeted in whole-group lesson
- Poses and discusses answers to high-level questions related to the text on leveled text

Small Group 2 (9:30–9:45)

Follow same strategies as small-group 1.

Small Group 3 (9:50–10:05)

Follow same strategies as small-group 1.

10:10–10:30   EIR Lesson

Follow EIR strategies. (Note that these students were also in one of the small groups.)

Regular Monitoring of Progress

Regular assessment of students' progress is important in their success in the EIR program and is a hallmark of effective teachers and schools (Lipson et al. 2004; Pressley 2003; Taylor et al. 2000). Teachers need to monitor students' reading abilities frequently to know when to fine-tune their instruction. They may need to provide more help or they may need to release more responsibility to the students to accelerate their reading growth. The teacher conducts an oral reading analysis to assess students' progress in word-recognition accuracy, word attack strategies, and fluency. (See Chapter 5 for this assessment.) The teacher also assessed students' abilities to summarize and write answers to questions on texts. (See Chapter 5.)

How the EIR Model Sits Within a Balanced Literacy Block

Now, let's look at how you might fit EIR lessons into your day by organizing your instruction around 90- to 100-minute reading blocks.

Reading Block: A Sample Schedule

Katie Tanner has a 90-minute reading block. She spends about 10 minutes a day on a whole-group minilesson on a reading comprehension skill or strategy that is a part of the school curriculum or state standards in reading. She spends about 55 minutes a day with three guided reading groups, whose members are usually reading a novel or an informational trade book, and 20 minutes on an EIR group (a second shot of quality instruction for her struggling readers). Her schedule appears on page 12. In the next chapter, you'll see how Katie and two other teachers make the content and pedagogy of effective reading instruction—and the principles of EIR—come alive in their whole-group and small-group lessons. This taste of their teaching will help you set the intervention lessons within a context. In Chapter 6, we'll also return to our three teachers' classrooms to see how they organize their day to provide EIR lessons to students who need more support and offer motivating independent activities to all their students.

DISCUSS WITH YOUR COLLEAGUES

1. Discuss aspects of effective reading instruction (content and pedagogy) you feel are embedded in your teaching. What aspects do you think are thriving? What do you feel less sure of? How might you improve your reading instruction?

2. What's the one thing that concerns you the most in regard to your teaching? Were there some things in this chapter that gave you insights into solutions to this problem?

Meet the Teachers

• •

The Differentiated Lessons and Teacher Collaboration That Support EIR

Katie Tanner, Eric Brown, and Maria Martinez, the teachers highlighted in this chapter, are connected to my work on effective instruction, school change in reading, and the EIR framework. Vignettes from their reading lessons are shared so that you can see how the teachers support and echo the reading content and pedagogy of reading and EIR lessons. You'll read the teachers' own words as they share the benefits of engaging in professional development with colleagues. Struggling fourth and fifth graders will excel farther if you take on EIR as a group, whether you team up with teachers at your grade level, in the intermediate grades, or as a schoolwide initiative.

The three teachers in this chapter teach in different schools with different student populations and needs; Table 2–1 highlights this diversity.

Diversity in the Highlighted Teachers' Schools

Teacher	Years Teaching	School Setting	Percentage of Students Who Receive Subsidized Lunch	Percentage English Language Learners
Katie	4	Urban	70	32
Eric	9	Suburban	41	18
Maria	25	Rural	53	5

Table 2–1 Diversity in the Highlighted Teachers' Schools

The Teachers

Katie teaches fifth grade at Randolph Elementary, an urban school where 70 percent of the students receive subsidized lunch and 32 percent speak English as a second language, primarily Somali and Spanish. Randolph Elementary is a diverse school, with about equal numbers of students who are European American, African American, Somali, and Hispanic. Katie has been teaching for four years, participated in study groups as part of a schoolwide reading improvement project for three years, and learned how to deliver EIR lessons through participation in an EIR study group in the third year of her school's reading improvement project. Katie's students grew by a mean of 7 normal curve equivalent points (NCEs) during the third year of the school-based reform effort, ending the school year with a mean NCE comprehension score of 53 (which corresponds to the 56th percentile).

Eric teaches fourth grade at Willard Elementary, a surburban school where 41 percent of the students receive subsidized lunch and 18 percent are ELL students from a wide variety of first language backgrounds. Eric has been teaching for nine years, and was new to Willard in the second year of his school's reform-in-reading project. He learned how to teach EIR intervention lessons in his first year at Willard. His students grew by a mean of 6 NCEs during fourth grade, ending the year with a mean NCE comprehension score of 55 (60th percentile, up from a mean NCE comprehension score of 49, or 48th percentile, in the fall).

Maria teaches fourth grade at Manona Elementary, a school in a small rural town where 55 percent of the students receive subsidized lunch and 5 percent are ELL students, primarily native Spanish speakers. Maria has been teaching for 25 years, and she learned how to teach EIR intervention lessons in the second year of her school's reading improvement process. In the third year of the school change project, Maria's students grew by a mean of 6 NCEs during the third year of the school-based reform effort, ending the year with a mean NCE comprehension score of 58 (65th percentile).

Common Factors in Students' Success

While these teachers have different styles and work in different settings, there are similarities in practices and recent changes to their instruction that are instrumental to the success of their teaching and the reading achievement of their students.

When asked what components were critical to the success of her classroom reading program and the changes to her instruction that made it more effective, Katie mentioned she is more confident about:

▶ Motivating students and engaging them

▶ Teaching students to focus on understanding what they are reading rather than just reading the words

▶ Getting kids to ask good questions and make more connections across disciplines

Katie also commented on the changes she's made in her reading instruction since the school began using the International Baccalaureate model (that focuses on the development of the whole child as an inquirer, both in the classroom and in the world outside):

▶ Using novels and nonfiction texts rather than basal texts and worksheets

▶ Incorporating required state skills into her work with novels or informational texts

▶ Having rich discussions about literature in which students connect to the world around them

For Eric, the success of his classroom reading program is attributed to:

▶ Focusing on how to teach students to become better readers

▶ Modeling, practicing, releasing, and cycling through good reading strategies in all types of reading

▶ Teaching students that becoming good readers is the goal, not how soon they finish particular tasks

Eric also commented, "My teaching of reading has changed unbelievably." Those changes include:

▶ Doing much more with small groups

▶ Stepping away from daily use of the basal reader and not worrying about starting at the beginning of the basal and going to the end

▶ Broadening his use of literature to develop comprehension and teaching more reading strategies

▶ Having student groups read chapter books and engage in deep conversations with one another

▶ Videotaping discussion groups and having students look at the tapes and talk about how to make their discussions more effective

Maria highlights the following instructional components as instrumental:

▶ Engaging students in high-level comprehension activities

▶ Motivating students through collaborative techniques

▶ Using EIR to meet the needs of struggling readers

She mentions the following changes in her reading instruction as crucial:

▶ Engaging students in instructional conversations

▶ Teaching reciprocal teaching strategies

▶ Introducing student book clubs

▶ Teaching EIR lessons to struggling readers

Teacher Talk

I share the teacher quotes that follow to encourage you as you embark on learning to teach EIR lessons as one aspect of your classroom reading program. Whether you are a beginning or veteran teacher, the implementation of EIR will help your struggling readers make good growth in reading during their fourth or fifth grade years. Here's what Katie, Eric, and Maria had to say when I asked them how professional learning, including EIR, changed their instruction.

The Influence of Collaborative Professional Learning on Teaching Practice

KATIE: Working together is important; we don't close our doors and hide like we might have in the past, but we get together, look at the research, and share ideas. We see that everyone is good at one thing or another. Working together in professional learning groups helps us use a common language, so our lessons are not confusing to the kids within grade levels and from one grade level to the next. Based on our professional learning efforts in the past few years, we now focus on kids' learning, not just our teaching. We are not teaching to teach; we are teaching to produce good learners.

ERIC: Our school has had study groups on EIR interventions and on comprehension strategies. The study groups encourage rigor, reflection, collaboration, and looking at cross-grade-level instruction. Reflection is a valuable practice that facilitates change and growth. If you value the ideas and methods of your colleagues, reflecting together can enhance your growth. We also have a literacy coordinator who helps guide us.

MARIA: Learning new teaching techniques can be a good thing. When we have the chance to collaborate, we share ideas and are very supportive of each other. Our learning together as a school has really changed how I teach reading. I am amazed when I look back at my first videotape, and see how far I've come in being a more effective teacher.

Biggest Benefits to Student Learning

When asked about the biggest benefits to student learning, again the teachers have similar responses.

KATIE: *I see higher engagement in reading and higher comprehension through book discussions and students' use of explicit reading strategies. With book discussions, I have to model a lot at the beginning of the year, but by the end they are good at it and really enjoy it. Their reading scores on the district test have gone up quite a bit, especially for my lowest readers. I think the EIR lessons have helped them a lot.*

ERIC: *I see growth in a lot of areas. My kids attain higher comprehension by using explicit reading strategies. Students can now identify strategies they use. They have a better understanding of higher-level questions, and they are better able to express their opinions and beliefs. They've been able to make good connections. Students are more excited about reading. Their scores have improved as well. I think a lot of it is teaching to their appropriate reading levels. EIR and small groups have helped with this. Also, at our data camps we talked about where we need to go with the kids to get them ready for fifth grade.*

MARIA: *Because of instructional conversations and book clubs, students understand their stories at a deeper level and are getting along better as well. If you come into my classroom now, you will see students writing about what they have read, relating to their own experiences, and reading books independently or with partners. Their discussions are amazing, even without my direction. The pure love of reading is evident. We do so much more partner and small-group work. Students are much more on task, but it is not a quiet room anymore. However, this tells me they are discussing and engaged, and they show a lot of enthusiasm. We are helping all students succeed, especially our EIR kids, but even our highest kids have improved quite a bit.*

On the following pages, detailed descriptions of these three teachers' reading lessons provide examples of what effective reading instruction looks like in practice. You will see how different teachers incorporate elements of effective reading instruction into their teaching based on their own styles and, of course, their students' needs. Notice how the teachers integrate the various components of content, including instruction in word recognition, fluency, vocabulary, and comprehension, as well as elements of pedagogy, including direct teaching and coaching; differentiation; and intellectually challenging independent, partner, and small-group activities.

Sample Lesson: Katie
Book Clubs

Katie wants her students to become independent readers and thinkers who are responsible for their learning. She feels the most effective way to do this is through book clubs; in fact, she does most of her reading instruction through book clubs whose members are reading novels and nonfiction books appropriate for their reading level.

Protocol

Students are typically allotted 10 days to read, provide written responses, and lead discussions about novels. Katie teaches important comprehension strategies (e.g., monitoring comprehension, summarizing, generating good questions for discussion) and state-mandated skills and strategies (e.g., understanding cause-effect or main idea), as well as techniques for participating in book club discussions, in whole-group minilessons at the beginning of each day's reading block and revisits these strategies and techniques during the book club meetings.

Although eight or ten students may be reading the same book, they discuss the book in subgroups of four or five, so more children have an opportunity to respond. Katie then meets with the whole book club, and the members share what they discussed in subgroups, make connections to skills and strategies covered in the whole-group minilesson, and prepare for independent work.

Students' independent work includes reading the next twenty pages of the book, writing a journal entry of their choice, and answering high-level questions that Katie (or the book club guide) posed. The students share their written responses with Katie one-on-one in between her small-group lessons or during the 30 minutes of independent work at the end of the reading block.

Whole-Group Minilesson on Cause-Effect Relationships

One day in February Katie asks her students, "What is a cause-effect relationship and why is it important?" Students define *cause* and *effect*. One student says, "We need to understand cause and effect so we understand what we are reading." A few students give examples from their lives. Katie gives every student a chance to respond by sharing with a partner a cause-effect relationship from the book their club is reading.

Book Club Discussions

The book clubs begin day 10 of their work on their book: *Turnabout* by Margaret Peterson Haddix, *Project Mulberry* by Linda Sue Park, or *That Crazy Eddie and the Science Project of Doom* by Judy Cox. These books connect to their science unit: All three books involve a science experiment of one sort or another, and the students are currently working on their own science projects as well.

Katie joins the group of above-average readers, who have just discussed their reading of *Turnabout* from day 9. She asks what went well in their discussion. Nate responds, "Our discussion was good." Katie prompts him to elaborate: "Can you tell us more about that?" Nate says, "We helped each other answer our questions." Students also share some of their responses to discussion questions and the cause-effect relationships they have found in their book. One boy offers, "They take the treatment and then they get younger." A girl says, "Anny Beth and Melly move into the hotel and then they run away to Kentucky." Katie prompts, "That's right, that is the sequence of what happened. What caused them to run away?"

At their seats, students are to read the last twenty pages of their book. Katie says, "Here's what I want you to do. Predict in writing what will happen. Do you think Melly and Anny Beth will return to the agency? How do you think the story will end?" Also, students are to write answers to several questions they will discuss during their next book club meeting: *Does the story have an uplifting ending? Why or why not? Is that how you predicted the book would end? What did you think about the ending to the book? Why? Would you take the injection to get younger? Why or why not? Pick a topic from the reading log list and write about it in your reading log.* (Every day, students choose one topic from the list and then cross it off so they don't write on the same topic twice for that particular book. Topics, as suggested by Raphael and colleagues [2002], include connecting my life to the book, character map, what would I do?, my favorite part and why, compare-contrast, critique, connection to the world around me, and questions to ask my group.)

For the next 30 minutes Katie meets with the groups reading *Project Mulberry* and *That Crazy Eddie and the Science Project of Doom*, following procedures similar to those described for the group reading *Turnabout* but adapting to meet students' needs.

Independent Activity

While Katie is meeting with the groups, the other students first complete independent work related to their book club reading. If they finish before the final segment of the reading block, they read for pleasure from a book of their choosing.

During the last 30 minutes of the reading block, students work independently on their science project, reading, researching the Internet, and writing. They also spend some time reading for pleasure from a book of their own choosing, on which they keep a log.

EIR Lesson

During the final 20 minutes of the reading block students who need more reading support meet with Katie for an EIR lesson.

Reflection

Katie provides excellent, differentiated instruction as she teaches a state-mandated comprehension skill in a whole-group lesson, which she then reinforces in guided reading groups. Her instruction is intellectually challenging, students' independent activities are motivating and require high-level thinking, and students are actively engaged. The lesson also encompasses collaborative work and student choice.

Sample Lesson: Eric

Using Summaries and High-Level Talk to Learn from Informational Texts

Whole-Class Lesson

Eric writes *summarizing* on the board and tells his students what this means. "Summarizing the important points is a very important skill. It shows that you comprehend what you are reading. I'm going to summarize for you what I did last night. I left school and I needed to grocery shop. I had seven things on my list, but when I got there, I didn't get just what was on my list. I paid for my groceries and went home. Now, who can summarize what they heard me say?" A student summarizes. Eric asks, "Did she use exactly the same words that I used?" Students answer no. "But did she do a pretty good job of summarizing what I did last night?" Students answer that she did.

Small-Group Work

Students, in pairs, each read a nonfiction story (one about a circus, the other about a fishing trip) aloud to the other. Both stories are short and easy to read and understand. The student who listens to the first story summarizes it. Then that student reads the other story aloud to his or her partner, who summarizes it. Eric circulates and provides feedback as the students read and summarize.

Differentiated Lesson for Lower-Ability Readers

Later Eric works again on summarizing with struggling readers in a guided reading group. "Today you are going to be reading a short article about desert life. Next year you will be reading more nonfiction in social studies, science, and health, and it is important for you to be able to summarize the main ideas and supporting details of what you read."

Together the group reads an article at their reading level about the saguaro cactus. After they have read the first page, looked at the picture, and read the picture caption, Eric models aloud how to summarize. "So now I'm going to think about what the main idea was on that page. This is what I come up with: "The saguaro cactus is important to desert animals. The saguaro is important because [he lists the reasons]. Okay, next page. Again I'm thinking: What is the most important idea on this page? Please follow along as I'm reading." Students chuckle as Eric reads. "I notice I have a couple photos to look at, and I need to make sure I read the captions. I'm going to think back to what I read on that page—what was the most important idea? Well, animals' bodies can change in order to protect them from the environment. So the main idea of what I read is that animals adapt to their environment. Here are some details."

Students read the next page on their own and talk aloud to a partner about the main idea and important supporting details. They finish the article independently, summarizing each page by writing the main idea and important details in two or three sentences.

Differentiated Small-Group Lesson for Average-Ability Readers

Eric meets with five students who have read a five-page section of a book at their reading level about severe weather. "Last time, we read about hurricanes, and we jotted down some big ideas. Now we're going to take these and put them into a summary." Eric points to the chart of big ideas the group had created earlier. "What idea should we start with?" A student says, "Hurricanes are powerful storms." Eric replies, "That's a good topic sentence." He writes this on the whiteboard. "Are there ideas on the chart I should eliminate because they're not big ideas?" A student suggests, "Severe flooding." Eric replies, "Let's talk about it. Explain why we should get rid of it." The student explains his reasoning. Eric asks, "What do the rest of you think about what he said?" They decide to keep the idea. Later Eric says, "I heard you say details. They are interesting. Do we want them in? What else should we add?" Students offer: "Destroy property." "Kill more people than any other extreme weather." They complete the summary to everyone's satisfaction. Eric then tells them that while they are working independently he wants them, with a partner, to write a summary for the next section of the text. He reminds them to clarify confusions and talk about vocabulary as they read.

Differentiated Small-Group Lesson for High-Ability Readers

Eric meets with six students who are reading a book at their reading level about creatures of the dark. Students have read the book on their own and summarized sections of text on sticky notes. They have also marked the places that they need to clarify and vocabulary that they would like to discuss in the group.

One student reads his first sticky-note summary aloud. Eric asks, "What do you think? Does he tell what it was mostly about?" Students agree that he has. Two other students read their summaries. Eric asks, "Why is what we're doing important?" Students reply, "So we understand the material."

Next Eric says, "Let's share spots needing clarification. What does that mean?" A student volunteers, "This is a spot you don't understand or don't know." Eric elaborates: "Yes, and *clarifying* means to clear it up. Go to page 6. Is there anything you needed to clarify there?" Students don't know the word *tapetum*, and together they find out what it means. Then they glance at pages 10 through 13 and predict with a partner what they will be learning about next. Then with a partner, they read and summarize these pages, clarify things they don't understand, and generate "thinking" questions for discussion.

This lesson is an excellent example of exploring informational text through collaborative learning activities. It is also a good example of differentiated instruction.

Whole-Group Lessons on Using Multiple Strategies

After working on summarizing for a month in the fall, Eric focuses on teaching his students to use multiple comprehension strategies as they are needed. (See a discussion of *transactional strategies instruction* in Chapter 4.) In addition to summarizing, students have learned to generate "thinking questions" for book clubs. They also regularly talk about comprehension monitoring, or clarifying confusions, and they make predictions when it makes sense to do this.

Sample Lesson: Maria
Instructional Conversations (*see Goldenberg 1992*)

Whole-Group Lesson

Maria asks, "Why do we have instructional conversations?" Students respond: "So we understand the story better." "So we hear others' opinions." Maria elaborates, "It leads us into exploring the big picture. I want you to use prior knowledge. Talk in your small groups about conversations you've had outside school." Maria moves around the room, listening to the groups. She asks one group, "How are these conversations different from those we have here in reading class?" A student answers, "We talk about other things, not about a book." Maria asks, "How are they the same? Share your ideas with your group."

Continuing to circulate, Maria asks another group, "How are you going to use instructional conversations in the future to make you a better reader?" Students say they'll use them in book club to compare the current story with others they've read.

Reconvening the class, Maria asks students to turn to a partner and share which behaviors they think are necessary in order to have an instructional conversation. She then forms a "fish bowl" group to talk more about how to have good conversations while the rest of the class observes and takes notes. She asks the fish bowl group a question about a character in the story the class read last week. A student gives a detailed answer. Another student responds to what the first student said. A third student agrees with the second student. The remaining student contributes his ideas. All the students support their comments with examples from the story.

When the fish bowl group finishes their conversation, Maria asks for compliments from the observers. Students offer: "They were still." "They stayed on topic." "They looked at each other." "They didn't interrupt." "They were polite." Maria asks the observers if they have any suggestions. Students answer: "They could have looked back in the text more." "There was some fidgeting." Maria says, "Overall, they did a pretty great job. What do we want to keep in mind in our conversational groups?" Students respond: "Be like the model group." "Stay on topic." "Move on."

Small-Group Work Within the Whole-Class Lesson

Maria divides the class into two groups. Each group begins instructional conversations about the story "One Grain of Rice" by Demi based on questions that they wrote on a discussion sheet. The student leader of each group asks for all students' input and gives feedback like, "I never thought of that before," and "That's a good answer."

Maria listens as the students respond to one another's questions and answers. She prompts the leader of one of the groups to move on to another question. A student then asks, "What would you do with the rice if you took it?" The student leader answers first, then others share their ideas. The student leader then calls on specific students, asking if they have any input.

Maria moves on to the second group. The leader has just prompted a student to ask a new question, which is, "Would you like to be the Raja? Explain." A student answers, explaining his reasoning.

Next Maria asks both groups to discuss what went well and how they might improve. Maria listens as the groups evaluate themselves, then summarizes for the whole class. "I heard comments like, 'Look at me when I speak,' 'Some are saying too much,' and 'Not everyone participated.' These are good evaluative comments." She reminds students to also talk about what went well—she wants to hear their successes. Maria concludes by praising them for a job well done and by summarizing what they might do better next time.

Partner Work

Maria sends students back to their desks and points to a question she has written on the board: "Talk with your partner about the last time you used a written response to help you understand something. How can writing about what we read make us better readers?" Student partners share their ideas as Maria circulates and listens in. A boy says, "It helps you understand a lot of other stories better because you can compare." His partner says, "You can check what you write." Maria prompts them to elaborate: "How can writing help you understand the big picture?" As these two students start talk about this, Maria asks another pair the same question.

Next Maria discusses a theme of "One Grain of Rice"—being greedy—and models connecting the main character, the Raja, with this theme. She also tells about her own experience with being greedy. Then students, in pairs, talk about a time they have been greedy or when they have seen someone be greedy and share their thoughts about how their experience relates to the Raja's actions.

Finally, Maria points to another question on the board, "What lesson does 'One Grain of Rice' teach us?" She wants the students to answer this question in writing, but first, she asks them to talk it over with their partner. Circulating, Maria asks one pair, "What kind of person is the Raja?" The two students tell her their ideas. Maria repeats this question to several more pairs, listening to their responses.

Independent Work

Students individually begin writing their responses to "One Grain of Rice," discussing the theme or identifying a lesson they think the story is teaching. They use a four-point rubric as a reference point in order to make their writing better (see Chapter 5). When they finish, they read quietly to themselves. Some students complete book reports on a response sheet.

Differentiated Support

At a back table, Maria provides additional support to four students as they write their responses. "What does this story teach us?" she prompts. One girl asks, "Is this how you spell *greedy*?" Maria tells her they'll fix spelling later and asks, "How do you know the story is about being greedy? What are examples from the story?" The girl begins writing. Maria shows a boy a sample response and explains how it gives specific examples from the story. He begins writing. Reading over another student's shoulder, Maria tells her to break up a long sentence. She tells the final member of the group that he has very good supporting details and now needs to come up with an ending. He says with enthusiasm that he knows how he will conclude his response and gets busy writing.

Reflection

Maria's lesson contains good examples of high-level talk and writing about text. She regularly offers positive, enthusiastic feedback. She also provides differentiated instruction to students who need more support in writing their responses. Students are actively engaged as they work with a partner, in small groups, and on their own.

Schoolwide Dimensions of Effective Reading Instruction and EIR Interventions

In addition to the many aspects of effective classroom instruction discussed above, teachers need to consider aspects of their schoolwide reading program. Take a moment to think about your own school, and how you might collaborate with one or more of your colleagues to implement EIR within a shared vision of effective reading instruction.

The best teaching possible arises from schools in which teachers develop a shared set of understandings and beliefs about teaching and learning in general, and teaching reading in particular. Considerable research in the last decade has identified the following characteristics of schoolwide reading programs that support teachers' abilities to increase students' reading abilities. These schools have:

▶ a unified vision for teaching reading in every grade and a cohesive, schoolwide program (Taylor, Raphael, and Au, in press; Taylor et al. 2005)

▶ a substantial number of minutes and designated blocks of time devoted to reading instruction across the grades (Taylor et al. 2000)

▶ a schoolwide assessment plan in which student data are collected and used regularly to inform instruction (Pressley et al. 2003; Taylor et al. 2000; Taylor et al. 2002)

▶ interventions in place to meet the needs of students who are experiencing reading difficulties, who have special education needs, and who are English language learners (Foorman and Torgesen 2001; Mathes et al. 2005; Taylor et al. 2000)

▶ effective parent partnerships (Edwards 2004; Taylor, Pressley, and Pearson 2002)

An individual teacher working hard on her own to enhance her practice can make a huge difference in the lives of the students in her class. And yet, it is ideal to have an effective schoolwide reading program in place, whereby a common vision, time to work together, and a culture of peer support are part of your school's DNA. As Katie, Eric, and Maria, and so many other teachers attest, working with colleagues can provide amazing support. It's hard to examine and critique your own practice. Trusted colleagues can watch you teach, give you feedback, point out your strengths, and offer ideas to enhance your instruction in certain areas. This support helps you look closely at your practice, make modifications, and in the end, teach as effectively as possible so all of your students become skilled, motivated readers.

I hope that you carry this overview of effective reading instruction with you as you read about EIR strategies in the next chapter. You might also want to explore the content, pedagogy, and interpersonal skills of exemplary teachers further. Professional books and research articles abound on many of the components of effective reading instruction discussed in Chapters 1 and 2. (Also see pages in the endmatter for Recommended Professional Readings.)

DISCUSS WITH YOUR COLLEAGUES

1. Discuss each of the three teachers described in this chapter. What do you like about their lessons? What questions do you have? As a group, is there one strand of effective reading instruction you would like to explore more?

2. Discuss instructional ideas you might try after reading about Katie, Eric, and Maria.

3. Discuss aspects of effective reading instruction (content and pedagogy) you feel are embedded in your teaching. Which aspects do you think are thriving? Which do you feel less sure of? How might you improve your reading instruction?

The Five-Day Lesson Routine

Now, it's time to look at the daily routines of the EIR lessons, the rationale behind them, and some basic getting started information. But first, let's review a few foundational ideas:

▶ With EIR, students' reading progress is accelerated because your instruction is based on the same effective reading instruction you use with *all* students—this is not about remediation.

▶ Students who are struggling with reading are given an extra shot of quality, small-group reading instruction. These children are getting this support in addition to, not instead of, other whole-group, small-group, and one-on-one attention.

▶ Engaging children's books are selected for the lessons (see the sample book list in Figure 3–1 on page 32 and on the DVD) to guide you.

▶ Fourth or fifth graders who need continued support in word-attack strategies for multisyllabic words are given the help they need. Additionally, many children who had a slow start in learning to read in the primary grades need to work on their reading fluency. Many also need to work on their reading. However, the focus is on improving reading comprehension while maintaining students' word-recognition accuracy and reading fluency.

Getting Started: FAQs

In Chapter 5 you will find more information about how to determine which children might benefit from EIR. For now, here are some questions teachers commonly ask about setting up the groups.

How many students are in a group?

Each group should have about five to seven students, seven being the maximum. If there are more than seven children in your room who need EIR lessons, I would recommend finding a way to have two groups instead of just one. If you have a reading resource teacher at your school, perhaps he or she can work with one group and you can work with the other. Then you can periodically switch groups so you have a sense of the strengths and weaknesses of all your struggling readers.

Who should teach the EIR students?

As hard as it is to teach two EIR groups, should you find you need to do this, I cannot recommend that an instructional aide teach one of the groups. Children at risk of reading failure desperately need quality, supplemental reading instruction, which is in addition to the regular reading program, and which is provided by certified teachers.

What advice do you have in regard to English language learners and EIR?

Often the question comes up as how to handle English language learners (ELLs) and fall placement in EIR. I would put the ELLs in an EIR group in the fall. I have found that ELLs generally do well in EIR (Taylor 2001).

How do students in special education fare with EIR?

I have also found that EIR works well with students who have learning disabilities. No modifications to the program are recommended.

However, students who are developmentally and cognitively delayed learn well in EIR, but easier texts are typically needed than those used in regular EIR lessons to keep the children feeling successful.

Do the children in EIR groups feel stigmatized?

Over the many years I've been implementing and researching EIR, teachers report that children do not feel stigmatized. In fact, children love the fast pace, interesting texts, and feelings of success they experience in EIR lessons. Children who no longer need the program often do not want to give the group up. All children are in small groups with their teacher, so no one seems to think much about who is with the teacher when. But the children in EIR lessons like the extra time with the teacher if she is the one teaching the EIR group.

What's the optimum time of the year to start EIR?

It's best to begin EIR in October. However, if you have just bought or been given this book and it is February, then for you, February would be the best time to begin. (It's just not a good idea to start any later in the year than March.)

What's the best way for me to begin to build my confidence with EIR?

After you read through the five-day procedures in Figure 3–1, read the Day 1 procedures again and watch the corresponding Day 1 video clips on the accompanying DVD. Soon, the EIR routines will seem very natural, and, as many teachers have reported, you will feel that the extra work on your part is worth the effort! For the past 15 years, I have consistently found that teachers, by February, are very excited about the progress they see their struggling readers making.

How do I know when I am ready to teach the lessons?

Once you have read this book, you may not feel completely ready to conduct the lessons, but I have found the best way to learn about EIR procedures is to just jump in and try them. If you have questions, and I'm sure you will, you can reread parts of the book or rewatch particular video clips. Ideally, you will be working with a group of colleagues learning and implementing EIR together so that you can share successes and discuss questions and uncertainties together. For additional expert support, go to www.earlyinterventioninreading.com.

Cross-Age Tutoring (or Partner Work)

Ideally, EIR instruction is done within the context of a cross-age tutoring program in which fourth-/fifth-grade students tutor second-/third-grade EIR students—or any younger second-/third-grade students who need reading support. The fourth or fifth graders meet for 20 minutes a day for three days to prepare to work with younger students on the fourth day. On the fourth day, they read an informational picture book or section of a longer informational book to their younger students and listen to the second/third graders read their own EIR story or other text. On the fifth day, the fourth/fifth graders most typically use the word-recognition, vocabulary, and comprehension strategies they have been practicing with their EIR books as they read from grade-level classroom textbooks. This work on Day 5 helps to build their confidence reading grade-level material.

Teachers report that the cross-age focus of the grades 4/5 EIR model appeals to their students and gives them a reason for working on their reading other than "to catch up because they are behind." Also, these students are proud to have been selected to work with younger students in reading and look forward to and enjoy working with their tutees. Research supports the efficacy of cross-age tutoring efforts as well (Guzetti 2002).

If you are unable to set up the cross-age tutoring component of EIR lessons, then on Day 3, students work with a partner in the EIR group instead. They reread their story to one another, discuss the questions they generated, and talk

Grades 4/5 Basic EIR Procedures

DAY 1 LESSON

1. The teacher activates background knowledge and has students read the first few pages of a new informational book on their own.

2. The teacher models and coaches in decoding multisyllabic words as students are reading. The teacher and students discuss word meanings in context.

3. The teacher coaches for comprehension on questions that engage students in high-level thinking.

4. Students finish reading or practice rereading their new book or book segment. This could be done at a later time in the day if time does not permit.

DAY 2 LESSON

1. The teacher and students practice the reciprocal teaching model with a few pages of text.

2. The children practice rereading their book as the teacher coaches in word recognition, providing help with multisyllabic words.

3. The teacher explains how to use the individual take-home sheet (see Figure 3–8), which prepares students for working with their younger partners (or EIR partner). Fourth graders work with second graders; fifth graders work with third graders. (Students can work with a partner in their EIR group if working with younger students isn't possible.)

DAY 3 LESSON

1. Students, with teacher support, practice reciprocal teaching with additional pages in their informational book.

2. The teacher gives students feedback on the take-home sheet. You should have students complete this sheet on Day 3 if it is not sent home.

3. Students practice reading their second- or third-grade EIR reading buddy's book (if available) so they are sure they can successfully coach their younger partner.

4. The teachers and students discuss strategies for coaching second or third graders.

5. Students practice reading their grade 4/5 book if they indicate on their take-home sheet that they need more practice. The teacher can conduct an oral reading analysis or an oral reading fluency check at this time.

However, if the cross-age tutoring piece is not in place, have EIR partners coach one another as they take turns reading their story and use their take-home sheets to discuss vocabulary and talk about the story.

DAY 4 LESSON

1. Fourth/fifth graders read their informational text to their second- /third-grade partners.

2. Fourth/fifth graders work with second/third graders on comprehension and vocabulary from ideas on their individual take-home sheets.

3. Fourth/fifth graders listen as second/third graders read their EIR story and coach as needed.

DAY 5 LESSON

1. The teacher and students discuss the partner reading experience from the previous day. They talk about things that went well, share problems, and talk about solutions to problems.

2. Using a text at their grade level, the teacher and students read a short selection and practice the reciprocal teaching model or focus on attacking multisyllabic words, discussing vocabulary, summarizing, and/or answering thought-provoking comprehension questions.

There are several other activities to choose from for Step 2 as well. Students can engage in independent reading as the teacher conducts an oral reading analysis or oral reading fluency check on one or more students. Or, the teacher can assess students' abilities to write summaries for short texts or to write answers to high-level thinking and comprehension strategy questions. Remember, you will spend two days on Day 5 activities (skipping Day 4 activities) if the cross-age tutoring component is not in place.

Figure 3–1 Grades 4/5 Basic EIR Procedures

about the meanings of the vocabulary they identified on their take-home sheets. Day 5 activities are completed on both Day 4 and Day 5 if you are not able to do the cross-age tutoring.

A Word About Using EIR Books

The children all work on the same book for the week. In the basic grade 4/5 model, all the books are informational. The teacher selects relatively short books that will appeal to second and third graders as well as fourth and fifth graders and are written at a third- to fourth-grade reading level. (See Table 3–1 for a list of exemplar books for the grades 4/5 program.) More on selecting books for EIR lessons can be found at the end of this chapter.

Table 3–1 Grades 4/5 Exemplar Informational Books

Keep in mind that these books should be at a third- to fourth-grade reading level and appeal to second-/third-grade reading partners.

Book Title	Author
Sea Turtles	Elizabeth Laskey
The Water Cycle	Bobbie Kalman
A Picture Book of George Washington	David Adler
Bengal Tigers	Theodorou
Dolphins	Richard and Louise Spilsbury
Flash, Crash, Rumble, and Roll	Franklin Branley (A Let's Read and Find Out Science Book)
Germs Make Me Sick	Melvin Berger (A Let's Read and Find Out Science Book)
Snow Is Falling	A Let's Read and Find Out Science Book
South America	A New True Book (Grollier)
Polar Bears: A True Book	Ann Squire
Look What Came from China	Miles Harvey

Table 3–1 Grades 4/5 Exemplar Informational Books

Overview of the Five-Day Lesson Steps

To recap, the weekly model shifts students to working with a second or third grader on Day 4 (or EIR partner on Day 3), which boosts their confidence as capable readers and mentors:

▶ Students have three days of 20-minute, small-group instruction with a relatively short informational book that is written on about a year below grade level. Instruction focuses on practicing the steps of the reciprocal teaching model. Attention is also paid to decoding multisyllabic words and discussing the meanings of unfamiliar words.

▶ Ideally, one day is devoted to reading the practiced book to a younger student and tutoring this child on their own EIR text.

▶ One day focuses on application of EIR strategies to classroom textbooks (or two days may focus on this if the cross-age tutoring is not in place).

1. The teacher activates background knowledge and has students read the first few pages of a new informational book on their own.

2. The teacher models and coaches in decoding multisyllabic words as students are reading. The teacher and students discuss word meanings in context.

3. The teacher coaches for comprehension on questions that engage students in high-level thinking.

4. Students finish reading or practice rereading their new book or book segment. This could be done at a later time in the day if time does not permit.

Day 1, Steps 1 and 2: Read a Few Pages of the Text and Work on Word Recognition and Vocabulary

(10 min.)

As you and your students begin reading the book, spend a minute or two asking questions related to the book's subject to activate their background knowledge. Have your students read the first few pages of the book (students can finish reading this section of the text on their own in step 4 or later in the day); tell them you will come back to words that they had a hard time decoding or vocabulary that they did not know.

ſee it iN ActioN

Activate Prior Knowledge

Before students read *Germs Make Me Sick,* Rochelle asks them what they know about germs. Students offer ideas about times they have been sick. Students then read a few pages of their text on their own.

After students have read one or two pages, teach word-recognition strategies as children point out words they don't know. Remind other students not to call out a word if you are working with one child on decoding. Use a consistent strategy for attacking multisyllabic words (see Figure 3–2; also see Taylor et al. 1995). Remind students regularly that this is a strategy they can use when they are reading on their own. The strategy works best with words already in students' listening vocabulary, and many of the words struggling readers come

Strategy for Decoding Multisyllabic Words

1. Break the word into chunks (approximate syllables) with one vowel (or vowel team) per chunk.

2. Be flexible as you sound out the chunks, especially the vowel sounds. If one sound doesn't work, try another (see the Advanced Vowel Chart in Figure 3–3).

3. Remember to use context clues.

4. After you sound out the chunks, try it again only faster.

5. Remember that this will only get you close to the right word. Keep thinking of context.

Figure 3–2 Strategy for Decoding Multisyllabic Words

across in their EIR texts will, in fact, be words in their listening vocabulary because the books are slightly below grade level.

It really doesn't matter if the students break a word into the exact syllables as found in the dictionary. Instead, they need to know that a chunk, or an approximate syllable, has one vowel or vowel team per chunk. They need to learn to be flexible with their sounding out of syllables and blending syllables together. They should be given a copy of the advanced vowel chart (see Figure 3–3) to help them remember the most common sounds for a particular vowel or vowel team. Consistently remind students that if one sound doesn't work, they should try another.

Also, remind students frequently that their sounding out will only get them close to the real word. As they are blending syllables together, they need to think of a word that is close to what they are saying and that makes sense in the text. I often find that children don't rely on context enough as an additional support when they are sounding out multisyllabic words.

Teaching Vocabulary

Beck, McKeown, and Kucan (2002) discuss the importance of talking about word meanings at point of contact in the text. As the group comes to words not in their listening vocabulary while they are reading their EIR book, stop to talk about the meanings of these words. When possible, ask the children to give an approximate meaning for a word by using clues in the text. In this case, part of the discussion should focus on what clues were used to try to figure out a word meaning. However, it is important to keep in mind that using context clues is not an easy task for students; available clues may be insufficient to determine a

Advanced Vowel Chart

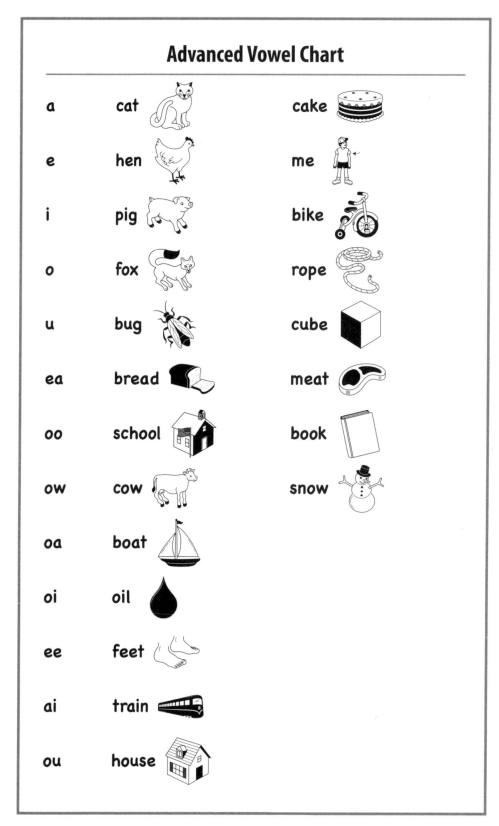

a	cat		cake	
e	hen		me	
i	pig		bike	
o	fox		rope	
u	bug		cube	
ea	bread		meat	
oo	school		book	
ow	cow		snow	
oa	boat			
oi	oil			
ee	feet			
ai	train			
ou	house			

Figure 3–3 Advanced Vowel Chart

word's meaning. If there are not sufficient context clues for an unfamiliar word in the text you are reading, tell students the word's meaning, or help them look it up in the dictionary.

See it in Action

Decode and Discuss Words

After Rochelle's students have read the first few pages of *Germs Make Me Sick*, they stop to talk about words that they were not sure how to decode. Several students point to *microscope*. Rochelle writes the word on the board and asks, "What do we need to do to figure out this word?" Students say, "Break it into chunks." Students come up with mi/cro/scope, and Rochelle underlines the chunks as the students say them. They put all the sounds for the chunks together and say the word correctly. Rochelle asks if they know what a microscope is and the students say they do. Ashley reads a sentence, skipping over the word *viruses*. Rochelle says that skipping the word and reading on can be a good strategy, because you may find clues about the word and its meaning. The students sound out *viruses* by breaking it into chunks. Rochelle asks Ashley to reread the sentence to try to figure out what the word means. They decide the word *germs* is a clue that viruses get in your body and make you sick.

Day 1, Step 3: Coaching for Comprehension

(5 min.)

The notion of coaching children for understanding should guide discussions of the text they read. In my research, I have found that limited higher-level questioning occurs in the elementary grades but a focus on high-level talk and writing about text increases students' reading abilities (Taylor et al. 2000; 2003; 2005; 2007). The purpose of coaching for comprehension is to ask questions that stretch the children's thinking and get them to think and talk about things in the text that they may not have noticed on their own. Through these prompts, students interpret the text, relate a concept in the text to their own lives, and make other connections that deepen their understanding. Since high-level questioning occurs on other days as well, you need to remind the

Coaching for Comprehension:
Questions and Prompts for Teachers (Informational Texts)

The purpose of coaching for comprehension is to *expand* students' understanding of what they have read—rather than assess it. High-level questions are engaging, challenging, and require students to pause and think before answering.

Through Your Questioning, Students:

▶ Summarize the man ideas of all or part of the text.

▶ Stretch their understanding of the text by asking them interpretive questions.

▶ Relate the text to their lives.

Interpretive Questions

1. What did you learn from this material?

2. What questions do you have?

3. What would you like to learn more about?

4. Why do you think the author gave the title he or she did to the text?

5. What do you think are three main ideas (or the most important ideas) in this text?

6. For each main idea, what is an important supporting detail?

High-Level Questions That Relate to Children's Lives

Ask questions that are based on a concept in the text that relates to children's lives:

1. How does what you read about relate to our city (or state)?

2. Can you give examples of similar events in the world today?

3. Can you compare anything in this text to [another text] [something they have done in the classroom]? Why do you think these are similar or different?

4. What did you like, or not like, about this material? Why?

Figure 3–4 Coaching for Comprehension

children that not all of them will get to answer on each day. However, if the children are eager to share their ideas, they can talk with a partner.

Examples of questions to coach for comprehension are shown in Figure 3–4. It is important to keep in mind that the questions are only examples of the kinds of questions that you might ask to stretch children's thinking about the texts they are reading.

See it iN ActioN

Coach for Comprehension

After students have read the first few pages of the book and discussed unfamiliar words, Rochelle asks them, "What have you learned about germs that you did not know before?" Ashley offers, "They come in different shapes." Rochelle coaches for comprehension: "How do you think different shapes are going to affect us?" Ashley uses the picture to try to explain: "One type is bigger than another." Rochelle coaches, "What if you have one type of virus or another?" Ashley smiles and points to the picture as she says, "This one could be for colds, this one for the flu." Rochelle asks the other students if they think this makes sense and they nod in agreement. She concludes by asking, "Do you think we'll learn more about this? Would you like to?"

Day 1, Step 4: Finish Reading (or Reread) Text
(5 min.)

On their own, students finish reading or reread the text. As children practice rereading the EIR book they will later read to a second- or third-grade child (or EIR partner), they are working on their fluency. Because they want to do a good job reading to their younger partners, they have a reason to take this practicing seriously.

1. The teacher and students practice the reciprocal teaching model with a few pages of text.

2. Children practice rereading their book as the teacher coaches individuals in word recognition, providing help with multisyllabic words.

3. The teacher explains how to use the individual take-home sheet (see Figure 3–8), which prepares students for working with their second- or third-grade (or EIR) partners. Fourth graders work with second graders; fifth graders work with third graders. (Students can work with a partner in their EIR group if working with younger students isn't possible.)

Day 2, Step 1: Practicing Reciprocal Teaching
(15 min.)

The reciprocal teaching model was developed by Palincsar and Brown (1984) for middle-grade students who can decode informational text fairly well but do not comprehend it well. A considerable amount of research (see Rosenshine and Meister 1994) has found the technique to be effective. Explain to students that this is a study strategy—a way to help them learn to study and glean the most important ideas from informational text.

Working in a group, the students carry out four procedures, or steps, with chunks of text (see Figure 3–5). (They take turns being the "teacher," which they find very appealing.) They should start with a paragraph at a time, but after two or three weeks, they should move on to a page or a section at a time. Midway through the year, they should start following the reciprocal teaching procedures individually, writing down their responses to each step and sharing them with others in the group at the end. They should be told that they are practicing a study strategy that they can use when reading on their own.

At first you will need to model for students how to come up with important questions, how to summarize, and how to clarify anything that is confusing.

Steps in Reciprocal Teaching

- Ask one or two important questions about the chunk of text and get answers.

- Summarize the important ideas of the chunk in two or three sentences.

- Clarify anything that is confusing (monitor comprehension).

- Make predictions (if any come to mind) about what will be read next.

Figure 3–5 Steps in Reciprocal Teaching

see it in Action

Review Reciprocal Teaching

Rochelle asks, "What is the first thing we do?" Cole answers, "Ask questions." Rochelle coaches for elaboration: "What kinds of questions will you ask?" Cole says, "Questions that are not in the book," and Rochelle again asks him to clarify what he means. Rochelle then asks, "Why else do you ask questions as you read?" Jessica says that she asks questions to make sure her second-grade buddy pays attention. Cole says, "You ask questions so you understand."

Next they talk about summarizing. Rochelle asks, "What do you include in a summary?" Kyla says, "The most important parts." Rochelle asks, "Why do you summarize?" When students have a hard time answering, Rochelle rephrases the question: "Does a summary help you when you read?" Students agree that it does, and Cole adds eagerly, "You try not to put everything in your summary." Rochelle coaches for elaboration by asking why. Cole replies, "It would be too long." Heather adds, "Some words may not be important."

Now Rochelle and her students talk about what you do after summarizing. Jessica offers, "You ask questions about what you don't understand." Ashley chimes in, "This is like clarifying." Rochelle complements Jessica, a shy child, for speaking up.

The group goes on to talk about the final step, predicting. Rochelle asks why predicting is important. Heather says, "You do them in literature circle." Kyla tries to explain: "If you do a prediction you can see if you are right in the next chapter." Since students are having a hard time with this, Rochelle elaborates by asking another question: "Do you think it helps you understand the story better?" Students agree that it does.

Over time, however, you will be able to release responsibility to the children for these tasks and assume the role of a coach who provides support.

Asking Important Questions

Suggest children begin important questions with *how* or *why*. If they ask *what*, *where*, or *when* questions, gently remind them that the question is supposed to be about a big idea and not a "picky" detail.

Summarizing

You can help children summarize by limiting the number of sentences they can use. For a paragraph, tell them to come up with one sentence that states the most important thing they think the author is trying to communicate. For several paragraphs, a page, or a section of text, limit them to just two or three sentences in which to tell the most important ideas the author is trying to get across.

Summarizing is very difficult for children, and they need lots of practice (which they get throughout the year in the EIR program). For one thing, children do not look at text in the same way an adult does. What is important to them is often what is most colorful or interesting. However, by grades 4 and 5 they need to focus on things they learn from the text. This requires learning how to understand the most important ideas an author is trying to get across. Tips for teaching students to summarize informational text appear on page 43.

Clarifying Confusions

This step is really monitoring comprehension. That is, the reader should notice when something doesn't make sense and do something about it, because the purpose of reading is to understand the text. By modeling how to monitor comprehension, the teacher helps students see that it is not only okay but *normal* for a reader to be confused occasionally. Children often have a hard time learning to notice and stop when something isn't making sense. Struggling readers in particular often have not learned to read for meaning or to expect reading to be meaningful. Once children learn to notice that something isn't making sense, they need to learn a few fix-up strategies to improve their comprehension (see Figure 3–6).

Making Predictions

This step is optional. Ask students to make a prediction about what they will read next if one comes to mind, but don't force it.

Day 2, Step 2: Reread the Book and Coach One Another
(4 min.)

Children often like to read their informational book to a partner on Day 2. They can practice coaching as one or the other gets stuck, just as they will have to coach when they listen to their younger buddies read their story later in the week. (If students will not be reading to a younger student, postpone partner reading until Day 3.)

Teaching Strategies for Summarizing Informational Text

1. Explain to the students that summarizing means being able to write or explain the most important ideas contained in a paragraph, a page, or a section of text. Tell them it is impossible to remember all the ideas in informational text so it is important to learn how to remember and identify the most important ideas.

2. Model how to read one paragraph, page, or section of informational text at a time and select two or three words from the paragraph, page, or section that reflects its topic. These are "about statements" (e.g., "This page was about elephant teeth.").

3. Model (talk aloud) how to turn the topic into a complete sentence that reflects the most important idea. Write the idea on the board. This is an "about statement." (If a page or section is used, write down one to three other important ideas.)

   Students have a tendency to write or tell too many ideas so it is important they learn how to limit the number of ideas. Ask, "What do you think are the most important ideas the author wanted you to remember?" Model to explain why certain ideas would not be good main idea statements because they are too general or too specific, and why others aren't important to write down or tell after the main idea. Repeat this process for a few more sections, until they are able to do a three- to five-page reading.

4. Model how to study from a written summary by reading it over and reciting the important ideas.

   Repeat this process as much as needed before the students write or tell their own summary statements.

   For guided practice, the teacher and students work together through several sections of text, summarizing while the teacher provides support as necessary.

   For independent practice, the students work alone or with a partner to summarize a section or two from the text in writing and then practice studying their summary. They can also work with a partner to orally summarize sections of text.

Figure 3–6 Teaching Strategies for Summarizing Informational Text

Fix-Up Strategies to Repair Comprehension

▶ Reread.

▶ Ask yourself a question about what is confusing you and reread to answer your question.

▶ Use context clues or the dictionary to figure out the meaning of a word you don't know.

▶ Use the strategy for decoding multisyllabic words or a long word you think you have not decoded correctly.

Figure 3–7 Fix-Up Strategies to Repair Comprehension

Day 2, Step 3: Discuss Take-Home Sheet

(1 min.)

In addition to practicing at school, children should take their book home for additional practice on Day 2. Teachers report that they have little trouble getting the children to return their books because they know they need to have them to read to their second- or third-grade partner.

At home, the children complete the individual take-home sheet (Figure 3–8). In addition to practicing their text and writing down how many times they read it, students write down one question on the sheet and two vocabulary words to discuss with their younger buddy (or EIR partner). A parent or guardian signs the take-home sheet to acknowledge that the work was done.

Individual Take-Home Sheet

Book Title/Author: _____

Name: _____

Parent or Guardian Signature: _____

Reading for Fluency

I practiced reading this informational text _____ times.

_____ I am ready to read it to my younger buddy (or EIR partner).

_____ I need to practice some more.

Discussion

Write down one question about the text that makes you think and that you and your partner can discuss.

New Words

Write down two words to ask or tell your second or third grader (or EIR partner) about (and what they mean).

Word 1

Word 2

Figure 3–8 Individual Take-Home Sheet

see it in Action

Practice Reciprocal Teaching

Rochelle first reviews strategies for figuring out hard words before students read pages 8 and 9 of their book to themselves silently. "As you come to words you don't know, what are you going to do?" Students offer: "Put it into chunks." "Ask did it make sense." "Go back and reread." "Look at the picture." Rochelle also asks students what they will do with their sticky notes, and they say: "Write down key words." "Write down important ideas." "Write down things you don't know."

As students read, Jessica asks Ashley for help with a word. Ashley coaches, "Are their any chunks?" After Jessica sounds out the chunks slowly, Ashley says, "Say it again faster." Jessica comes up with the word *scratches* and rereads the sentence the word is in.

After students have read pages 8 and 9, Rochelle asks who wants to be the "teacher" as they apply the reciprocal teaching steps to these pages. "Remember, the teacher has to make sure to include everyone at the table."

Cole is selected to be the teacher. He starts by asking whether anyone has a question. Heather asks, "Why do bacteria get in your skin?" Ashley answers, "From cuts or scratches." Cole remembers to ask other students if they have other ideas. Rochelle reminds Cole to ask whether anyone else has a question. He does, and Kayla asks one.

Cole then gives a summary of the two pages. "Germs are all around in the air and in your body. Sometimes your body keeps out harmful germs." Ashley compliments Cole: "That was good, Cole. I'll give you an A+." Rochelle asks students why they think this is a good summary. Jessica answers, "Because he gave all the important points." Rochelle prompts, "Did he go on and give us a lot of details?" Students say, "No." Rochelle continues, "Do you think this is what the author wanted us to remember?"

Cole then moves on to monitoring comprehension. "Does anyone have any questions that they don't know?" Ashley asks about the word *harmful*. Rochelle asks the group to read the sentence again—"Many germs are not harmful"—and they talk about what this means.

Then Cole asks for predictions about what they will read next. Jessica thinks they will read more about how germs make you sick, because on the next page there is another person who is sick. At the end of the discussion, Rochelle compliments Cole on doing a good job as leader and making sure everyone got a chance to talk.

1. Students, with teacher support, practice reciprocal teaching with additional pages in their informational book.

2. The teacher gives students feedback on the take-home sheet. You should have students complete this sheet on Day 3 if it is not sent home.

3. Students practice reading their second- or third-grade EIR reading buddy's book (if available) so they are sure they can successfully coach their younger partner.

4. The teachers and students discuss strategies for coaching second or third graders.

5. Students practice reading their grade 4/5 book if they indicate on their take-home sheet that they need more practice. The teacher can conduct an oral reading analysis or an oral reading fluency check at this time.

   However, if the cross-age tutoring piece is not in place, have EIR partners coach one another as they take turns reading their story and use their take-home sheets to discuss vocabulary and talk about the story.

Day 3, Step 1: Practice Reciprocal Teaching

(5 min.)

Since informational books will almost always be longer than can be covered in one or two days, have students practice the reciprocal teaching steps using another section of text.

Day 3, Step 2: Discuss Take-Home Sheet

(3 min.)

Review students' take-home sheets with them. Check to see that they have written a question to ask their second or third grader (or EIR partner) that will generate some discussion. Also make sure that they have selected vocabulary words that can be explained and that are not too easy or too difficult for their second or third grader (or EIR partner) to talk about with them.

Day 3, Step 3: Students Read Grade 2/3 EIR Book

(6 min.)

If at all possible, it is important to borrow copies of the EIR books the second or third graders will be reading to your fourth or fifth graders so the older children have a chance to practice reading these books. You don't want them to be in the uncomfortable position of not knowing a particular word and being expected to coach their younger partner. Teachers report that their fourth and fifth graders may have trouble reading the grade 2 or 3 story without practicing it first.

see it iN ActioN

Prepare for Partner Reading

Rochelle begins by saying, "Students, this is the book the second graders will be reading tomorrow when we buddy read with them. Let's read it now just so we are sure we are familiar with what they are going to be reading to us." The students chuckle as they take turns reading *Animals Should Definitely Not Wear Clothing.* Kayla helps Heather break *disastrous* into chunks. Rochelle asks Heather whether she knows what the word means. Heather isn't sure, but comes up with the correct meaning. Cole helps Ashley sound out *unnecessary.* At the end of the reading, Rochelle says, "We'll let you have a chance to partner read this again in just a little bit. What words do you think the students will have trouble with?" A few students mention the words they had trouble with themselves. Rochelle asks them to go around the circle and mention a strategy they could use with their younger reading buddies. They mention: "Does that make sense?" "Go back and reread." "Skip the word and come back." "Look at the picture." Rochelle explains that chunking may be hard for younger readers and that they will have to help their reading buddies with this.

Day 3, Step 4: Review Coaching Strategies

(1 min.)

Your students need to be aware of some strategies they can use when coaching their younger reading buddies. Teachers have found a sheet with prompts for partner reading works well. (See Figure 3–9.) As an alternative, some teachers have the children generate their own list of coaching prompts. You want the students to understand that if their second or third grader gets stuck, they should give a hint or two before they tell the child a word.

Prompts for Partner Reading

"It starts with . . ."
(child gives his reading partner the beginning sound)

"This part says . . ."
(child provides his partner with a rhyming part like *at* or *op*)

"Look at the picture . . ."

"Look at this word again . . ."
(if child who is reading misreads a word)

"Break it into chunks"
(if partner is a grade 3, 4, or 5 student)

Figure 3–9 Prompts for Partner Reading

ſee it iN ActioN

Review Buddy Reading Strategies

Rochelle turns the group's attention to strategies they should use when reading their EIR book to their reading buddies. "The last thing we need to remember is that as we are reading our books, what do we need to do?" Kayla mentions making sure their buddies are paying attention, and Cole mentions asking questions. Rochelle then tells students, "Jot down a question that you think that they would be able to answer but also a question that you think would help them better understand the text."

Day 3, Step 5: Reread EIR Text

(5 min.)

Give students a chance to reread their grade 4/5 EIR text one more time. It is important to save a few minutes of the lesson for this if some of the students indicated on their take-home sheet that they needed additional time to practice. If students do reread their texts, you can do an oral reading analysis (see Chapter 4) or an oral reading fluency check (see Chapter 5) on one student at this time.

If the cross-age tutoring piece is not in place, have EIR partners coach one another as they take turns reading the text. They should use the coaching prompts in Figure 3–9 if a partner gets stuck on a word. They then use their take-home sheets to discuss vocabulary and talk about the story.

Day 4
Lesson Routine

1. Fourth/fifth graders read their informational text to second-/third-grade partners. (Remember to spend two days on Day 5 instead if the cross-age tutoring piece is not in place.)

2. Students work with their reading buddies on comprehension and vocabulary from ideas on their individual take-home sheets.

3. Fourth/fifth graders listen to second/third graders read their EIR story and coach as needed.

On Day 4, the fourth or fifth graders work with their second- or third-grade partners for 20 minutes. Each time the pair is the same. In this way, friendships begin to build. Once in a while, a pair just doesn't seem to be a good match, and changes will need to be made if this happens.

Most teachers find it works best if students work with one second- or third-grade teacher on the partner reading. Usually, the older students go to younger students' room, but you may find other arrangements also work well. The older children need an adult (e.g., educational assistant, parent, or grandparent volunteer) in the room who can provide help if problems arise. They may need to be reminded to coach, not tell, when the younger child gets stuck on a word. They may need to be offered a suggestion to get a child back on track if he is not paying attention during the older student's read-aloud.

Fourth- and fifth-grade teachers report that they learn how to help their students be good tutors if they watch the tutoring sessions on occasion. If your students go off to the younger students' classroom, I recommend that you work with your principal to arrange to get coverage in your classroom so that you can attend these tutoring sessions.

Often teachers say they are already engaged in cross-age partner reading with an entire class and another class. If this is the case, I recommend that the EIR cross-age tutoring be a second opportunity for the EIR children to work with a younger child. In this way, their EIR tutoring is seen as something special and, consequently, motivating for them.

ʃee it iN ActioN

video
8

Partner Reading

In this video segment, we see Cole reading with two second-grade boys; he stops at the end of every page to ask questions. Heather helps her student with the word *unnecessary*. Rochelle moves from one group to another, watching and coaching as needed.

Day 5
Lesson Routine

1. The teacher and students discuss the partner reading experience from the previous day. They talk about things that went well, share problems, and talk about solutions to problems.

2. Using grade-level text, the teacher and students read a short selection and practice the reciprocal teaching model or focus on attacking multisyllabic words, discuss vocabulary, summarize, and/or generate and answer thought-provoking comprehension questions.

There are several other activities to choose from for Step 2 as well. Students can engage in independent reading as the teacher conducts an oral reading analysis or oral reading fluency check on one or more students.

Or, the teacher can assess students' abilities to write summaries for short texts not read before or to write answers to high-level thinking and comprehension strategy questions on these texts.

Day 5, Step 1: Debrief the Tutoring Session
(5 min.)

Teachers have learned over the years that it is important to provide support to their fourth and fifth graders in terms of working with a younger student. One way to do this is by having a discussion the day following the tutoring. For example, students might comment on successes: "My partner is reading better and learning longer words." "I read with expression so my partner pays attention." Questions might focus on problems: "What can I do when my partner doesn't listen to me?" "What should I do if my partner is moving around?"

Day 5, Step 2: Give Students Additional Reading Practice with Grade-Level Texts
(15 min.)

I recommend that the tutoring take place on Day 4 because three days is long enough to spend on one text and to get the children ready to read to their younger partners. However, because the purpose of EIR is to provide extra support in reading, students in the program should get the chance on Day 5 (or Days 4 and 5 if there is no cross-age component in place) to work on reciprocal teaching or simply word attack, vocabulary, and comprehension related to a grade-level text, such as their basal reader or a social studies or science text. This reading should be done silently, so the students practice reading in this mode. Ask students to jot down words they come across in their reading that they don't know how to decode or words that they don't know the meanings of. Discuss these words after students have read the text segment you've selected for them. Additionally, the teacher or students can summarize a sec-

fee it iN ActioN

Discuss Tutoring

Rochelle begins, "Students, let's talk about what happened when you were buddy reading. What strategies did you find you were using? Was there anything you did differently this time that you haven't done before?" Students take turns sharing strategies that they had used and had written down in their journals. Next Rochelle asks, "How did your students do with the big words in this story?" Cole says his student sounded them out on his own. Heather says she had to help her student sound out the big words and even tell her some of the words. Rochelle asks the students if they modeled how to sound out longer words. Ashley is not sure, so Rochelle models this again with the word *unnecessary*. They go on to talk about what they did to keep their students interested in the story. Students offer: "Ask questions and tell them to answer the best they can." "Say good job or nice try."

tion of their grade-level text and generate discussion questions that will stretch the children's thinking.

If you do not wish to do this additional reading from a grade-level textbook, you should still meet to discuss the previous day of tutoring with your students. One thing teachers have done in the past is ask the children to write about their tutoring session in a journal and then use what they have written as a basis for a discussion about their experiences.

Following the debriefing discussion, another alternative on Day 5 is to have the students read a book for pleasure, as opposed to reading from a textbook, for the remainder of the 20-minute EIR session. During this time, you can conduct oral reading analyses (see Chapter 4) or oral reading fluency checks (see Chapter 5) on one or more students.

One other assessment activity you can do on Day 5 a few times a year is to have students write summaries for short texts or to write high-level thinking and comprehension strategy questions using passages they have not read before. You can use the scoring rubrics described in Chapter 5 to monitor students' progress on these two types of reading comprehension tasks.

ſee it iN ActioN

video
10

Other Uses for Reciprocal Teaching

Rochelle says, "The last thing we're going to do today is talk about how we can use reciprocal teaching strategies in literature circles." The students have not talked about this before. Heather responds, "Putting words in chunks if we don't know them." Ashley talks about decoding long words. Rochelle coaches, "Those are good ways to figure out words, but I also want you to think about our study strategies. What is your assignment from your teacher in literature circles?" Kayla replies, "Bring our notebooks with our summaries." Rochelle asks, "What can you do with your literature circle book that you do in EIR?" The students discuss summarizing, predicting, questioning, and monitoring comprehension.

Rochelle concludes by asking, "One last thing before we go. How can you use this next year in your social studies class?" This, too, is a new discussion topic for them. Kayla responds, "Write our strategies on paper." Rochelle coaches for elaboration: "What do you do with them?" Kayla isn't sure, but Cole shares an idea: "Try to figure out words by ourselves." Rochelle coaches, "Let's go beyond words, Cole." Cole continues, "Write down the most important things."

EIR Book Selection Guides and Other Lesson-Planning Resources

Providing students with quality children's literature to read is an essential piece of effective instruction, and every EIR lesson relies on an engaging book. In this section, I give you guidance on how to select good books for the EIR model. However, I want to emphasize that you need to make your own choices and discoveries about the books you use in EIR lessons. Why? Because somehow, following anyone else's suggestions flattens the vitality of the teaching and learning. Go with your own expertise and interests and the curiosities and sense of humor of your students.

The books you use should be written at the second- to easy-third-grade-level for fourth graders and third- to fourth-grade level for fifth graders. The books should also appeal to the younger students to whom your students will read. Here are more guidelines to consider:

▶ Select about five or six informational picture books that can be read to a second-/third-grade EIR student in 10 to 15 minutes.

▶ Select about ten longer informational books that you can break into two parts and spend two weeks on each part. If your students are not able to read everything in the information books to their reading buddies due to time constraints, you can work with them on selecting the parts that they will read aloud.

In Table 3–1 and on the DVD, you will find an exemplar book list that will help guide you as you look for certain characteristics when choosing books for EIR. This list will assist your planning and carrying out the lesson steps. Remember, you do not need to use the books that are given; they are just examples.

Additional resources that will help you teach EIR lessons are available on the DVD. Materials include teaching charts, an individual take-home sheet, examples of independent activities for all students, and assessment directions and recording forms. Some of these resources were discussed in this chapter; others are described in Chapters 4 and 5.

Summary

Now that we have covered the basic grades 4/5 EIR procedures, we'll turn to a few other instructional strategies that support these daily lessons in Chapter 4. We'll also take a look at how to implement transactional strategy instruction with students using informational text or to engage students in discussions of narrative text that focus on high level thinking if you feel your students are ready for new challenges by January or later in the school year.

DISCUSS WITH YOUR COLLEAGUES

▶ Discuss the video clips you saw and the teacher's use of coaching to help children respond, regardless of whether the focus was on word recognition, vocabulary, or comprehension.

▶ Discuss ways in which you might set up cross-age tutoring between fourth and second graders or between fifth and third graders.

Additional Instructional Strategies

B y the second half of the school year, you may feel the students in your EIR group are ready for new challenges. If you decide to use any of the following research-based approaches to comprehension instruction, I strongly recommend you participate in ongoing professional learning sessions, or study groups, with colleagues who are also interested in learning or refining techniques to improve their classroom effectiveness. Chapter 7, which deals with ongoing professional learning, offers general suggestions you can follow in a series of study-group meetings on a specific comprehension topic (see Figure 7–5).

Reciprocal Teaching as an Independent Study Strategy

After your students have worked through the steps of the reciprocal teaching model under your guidance, you can teach them to use reciprocal teaching as an independent study strategy (Taylor and Frye 1992). Instructional suggestions for introducing this technique are provided in Table 4–1. In follow-up EIR professional learning sessions, discuss the successes and challenges you've had in introducing this technique. Share data on students' growth in using reciprocal teaching strategies.

At first, students can jot down their summaries and important questions, as well as things they need to clarify, in writing (see the written response sheet in Figure 4–1) and share these concrete ideas with a partner or small group. However, once they've become skilled at writing them down, they can sometimes generate summaries and questions and think through confusing parts in their heads. Keep reminding students that this is a way they can study a social studies or science textbook on their own.

Introducing Reciprocal Teaching as an Independent Study Strategy

WHAT	Today, instead of working in groups, we are going to work on reciprocal teaching strategies individually: asking ourselves questions, summarizing important points after reading, clarifying confusions during reading, and making predictions (if any come to mind) before continuing to read.
WHY	You won't always be able to work in a group, but you can always stop as you are reading to ask yourself important questions and answer them. You can also summarize important ideas of a section or page of text before you go on to the next section or page. If you do these things, you will better comprehend and remember the material. (Being unable to come up with a good question or two about a page or section of text or to summarize the important ideas is a good sign that you should go back and reread the page or section.)
WHEN	It is a good idea to use these reciprocal teaching techniques when you are studying for a test or when it is important that you really understand what you are reading in an informational book or textbook.
HOW	Read one section (or page) of our current book at a time. Write one important question and answer it. Write a two- or three-sentence summary of the section. If there is a confusing part or a prediction you have, jot it down along with its location. Do this for two or three sections (or pages). Then we'll share what we have done.

© 2011 by Barbara M. Taylor from *Catching Readers, Grades 4/5*. Portsmouth, NH: Heinemann.

Table 4–1 *Introducing Reciprocal Teaching as an Independent Study Strategy*

Transactional Strategies Instruction

A logical step after teaching students how to use reciprocal teaching is to help them become independent, strategic, self-regulated learners who are able to use different strategies at different times. The term *transactional strategies instruction* (TSI) (Bergman 1992; Brown et al. 1995) stems from the natural discussion about strategies that emerges when students talk together about things they did to better understand a text. Through TSI students learn why, when, and how to use many strategies to monitor their comprehension: getting the gist, predicting, visualizing meanings, summarizing information, thinking aloud, and problem-solving. (See the strategic questions in Figure 4–2.) As students read, they identify (e.g., jot down) places in the text where they chose and used a particular strategy. Then they talk in a group about what strategies they used at particular points and why.

Students who receive transactional strategies instruction have been found to (a) be more aware of using strategies, (b) use strategies more often, (c) learn more information from text, (d) exhibit richer comprehension, and (e) show greater gains on standardized comprehension and word study skills tests than students who have not received this instruction (Pressley 2006).

Pressley (2006) reported that half a year to a year of comprehension strategies instruction leads to increased student comprehension; however, it is difficult to teach comprehension strategies well. As teachers, we have to talk aloud about reading strategically, and this is not an easy thing to do; as skilled readers, most of the time we use strategies subconsciously. Also, we have to turn

---

Reciprocal Teaching Independent Response Sheet

Name: _____   Book: _____

A. Summarize pages _____: tell about what you read in just one or two sentences.

B. Generate questions: ask two important questions about what you read.

  1. (About something on page _____)

  2. (About something on page _____)

C. Clarify and check for understanding: note other ideas that you have questions about or vocabulary that you need to understand better.

  1. (About something on page _____)

  2. (About something on page _____)

D. Predict: write a prediction about what you think will be in the next section of the text (if a prediction comes to mind).

Repeat steps A – D for the next section of the text.

Figure 4–1 Reciprocal Teaching Independent Response Sheet

Strategic TSI Questions to Ask Yourself and Others

1. Generate gist and summary statements:

    What is this article about? (gist)

    How can I turn my "about" statement into one or two important ideas? (summary)

    (Hint: use the reciprocal teaching summarizing steps.)

2. Predict:

    What do I think will happen next? Why?

    Was I right (after reading further)?

3. Relate life and visualize:

    What does this section or this page make me think of?

    What picture do I (can I) make in my head?

4. Think aloud:

    What am I thinking and why?

5. Problem solve:

    I don't understand _____.

    What can I do about it? (Hint: use the reciprocal teaching fix-up strategies.)

Figure 4–2 Strategic TSI Questions to Ask Yourself and Others

responsibility over to the students as they talk about the meaning of text and the strategies they are using, and this too can be difficult. We may not be used to letting students do most of the talking. Therefore, it's important to share successes with, ask questions of, and brainstorm solutions to problems with our colleagues if we are to teach comprehension strategies effectively.

Action Steps

1. Model reading a section of text and pointing out the comprehension strategies you are using. (Since children at this age have more trouble with informational than narrative text, I recommend using informational text.)

2. Lead a discussion about the strategies you used as you were reading.

3. Have students, on their own, read a section of text and discuss the comprehension strategies they used.

4. Coach them and provide feedback.

5. Hold study-group meetings to discuss issues and progress in the implementation of TSI. Share data on students' growth in using comprehension strategies strategically and in your ability to teach TSI. (Figure 7–6 provides a framework for these meetings, along with additional suggestions.)

Prompting Higher-Level Thinking and Coaching for Comprehension

Research shows that students make greater gains in reading ability when their teachers stress higher-level thinking (Knapp 1995; Taylor et al. 2000; Taylor et al. 2003). Knapp and his associates studied 140 high-poverty classrooms in elementary schools in California, Ohio, and Maryland. They concluded that effective instruction emphasizes higher-order thinking much more than lower-order skills. Achievement was higher the more the teacher emphasized reading the text rather than drilling skills. Additionally, achievement was higher the more reading and writing were integrated, the more students discussed what they were reading, the more the teacher emphasized deep understanding of text rather than literal comprehension, and the more the teacher taught discrete skills within the context of reading.

The CIERA Beating the Odds study of effective schools and accomplished primary grade teachers (Taylor et al. 2000) found that in contrast to teachers in the least effective schools, teachers in the most effective asked more higher-level questions. Also, the teachers identified as most accomplished across all schools asked more higher-level questions than the teachers identified as least accomplished.

However, it appears that teachers generally ask more lower-level than higher-level questions. In the CIERA School Change Project (Taylor et al. 2003), lower-level questioning, on average, took place 47 percent of the time in grades 2 through 5. In contrast, higher-level questioning took place only 20 percent of the time. Nonetheless, asking higher-level questions was significantly related to students' reading growth during the school year.

To focus on higher-level talk and writing about text, try to use higher-level questions that typically require you to coach for comprehension (see the examples in Figure 4–3 and the theme-based questions in Figure 4–4). Have your students discuss rather than recite; don't ask rapid-fire questions requiring prompt, low-level responses. Try to stay out of the conversation as much as possible (or at least try not to do as much of the talking as the students); instead, look at yourself as a coach who is helping students express and/or clarify their ideas. Give the students enough wait time, and let them know you are interested in their ideas rather than in what they think you want to hear.

Action Steps

1. Meet with your colleagues to share successes, ask questions, and brainstorm solutions to problems as you learn how to more effectively engage students in higher-level talk and writing about texts.

2. Hold a study-group meeting once a month to discuss issues and progress in the implementation of more higher-level talk and writing about text. Share data on students' growth in engaging in higher-level talk and writing about text and in your ability to engage students in higher-level talk and writing about text. (Figure 7–6 provides a framework for these meetings, along with additional suggestions.)

3. Review Figure 4–3. Then look at a videotape of someone leading students in talk about text, look at the questions in a teacher manual, or look at questions someone prepared to engage students in talk about text. Discuss what makes a question (and students' responses to it) lower or higher level.

4. Discuss barriers to asking higher-level questions such as (a) it's hard for kids to wait while one student is talking; (b) if you break kids into small groups for discussion, they get out of control; (c) some kids want to do all the talking, and some never want to say anything; (d) some kids get off track and keep talking and talking; (e) it is hard to stop yourself from doing a lot of the talking yourself. Brainstorm solutions to some of these problems. Also discuss the advantages of asking higher-level questions that make it worth working on overcoming barriers.

5. Read "The Bear and the Crow" (Lobel 1981). Look at Figure 4–4 and discuss the pros and cons of each set of questions. Discuss the advantages of focusing on story theme.

6. Bring the questions you asked about a story or article during an EIR lesson to a group meeting, as well as the student responses. Talk about which questions stimulated higher-level thinking. What other questions could you have asked to stimulate higher-level thinking?

7. Videotape a reading group discussion and bring in a short segment (5 or 6 minutes) to discuss with your study group. (Use the video-sharing protocol in Figure 7–4.) Ask questions like the following to deepen your discussion: *What can you say about the children's engagement during the discussion? What questions seemed to stimulate the highest-level thinking? What are some other questions you might have asked to stimulate higher-level thinking? What are some*

Teacher Questions and Prompts to Stimulate Higher-Level Thinking

The purpose of coaching for comprehension is to *expand* students' comprehension of what they have read, not assess it. Higher-level questions are engaging and challenging and require students to pause and think before answering.

Through Your Questioning, Students:

▶ Summarize all or part of the story or nonfiction text.
▶ Stretch their understanding of the story by asking them interpretive questions.
▶ Determine the big idea of the story, its theme.
▶ Relate the story to their lives.

Examples of Questions to Coach for Comprehension

▶ Summarize the story. What happened at the beginning of the story? The middle? The end? (Answer in just a few sentences.)
▶ Why do you think Character X did Y?
▶ How did Character X change?
▶ What did you learn from this story?
▶ What did you like about this story?

Interpretive Questions Based on the Text

▶ What kind of person do you think (name of character) is? What in the story makes you think this?
▶ What are some good or bad things that happen in the story? Why do you think this?
▶ What is an important thing that happened in the story? Why do you think it is important?
▶ Why do you think the author gave the title he or she did to the story?
▶ What did you like best about (name of character)? Why? What in the story helped you think this way?
▶ What did you not like about (name of character)? Why? What in the story made you think this way?
▶ If you were the main character, would you have done the same things the main character did? Why or why not? What might you have done differently?
▶ Why do you think (name of character) did . . . ?
▶ How did (name of character) change? Why do you think this happened?
▶ What do you think were three main ideas (most important ideas) in this nonfiction article?

High-Level Questions That Relate to Children's Lives

Ask questions that are based on a concept in the story that relates to children's lives:

▶ Which character is most like you? Why?
▶ Which character would you like to be like? Why?
▶ Which character would you most like to have as a friend? Why? What in the story helped you make this decision?
▶ How are you like (name of character)? How are you different?
▶ How is (name of character) like a family member? How is the character different?
▶ Can you compare anything in this story to (name another story or something else you have experienced in your classroom that could be compared)? Why do you think these are similar (alike) or different?
▶ Ask nonfiction-type questions that relate to your state (e.g., Could you find these animals in our state? Do these events take place in our state? Why or why not?)
▶ What did you like (not like) about this story or article (nonfiction)? Why?

Figure 4–3 Teacher Questions and Prompts to Stimulate Higher-Level Thinking

Questions About "The Bear and the Crow"
(Lobel 1981)

Traditional Recitation with Some Higher-Level Questions

▶ How was Bear dressed at the beginning?

▶ What happened next?

▶ Describe how Bear was dressed after talking to Crow.

▶ What would you say about Bear's new outfit?

▶ What happened at the end?

▶ How did you feel at the end?

▶ What does the moral of the story mean?

Higher-Level Theme-Based Questions

▶ One possible theme of this story is being gullible. What does it mean to be gullible?

▶ Should Bear be pitied for being a gullible victim, or should he be laughed at for being a gullible fashionmonger?

▶ Was Crow a bully or was he just having some fun?

▶ Did Bear deserve people's laughter?

▶ Is being gullible being a victim or a fool?

▶ Can you think of another moral to the story?

Figure 4–4   Questions About "The Bear and the Crow" (Lobel 1981)

other ways you might have organized the students to encourage them to discuss what they had read?

8. Have a teacher bring in student writing samples from a lesson in which students were asked to write higher-level responses to what they had read. Use the looking-at-student-work-protocol (Figure 7–7) to guide your discussion of the student work. What can you say about the children's engagement during the writing activity? What questions seemed to stimulate the highest-level thinking? What are some other questions the teacher might have asked to stimulate higher-level thinking?

9. Audio- or videotape three or four class sessions or ask a consultant or a peer to observe you and code the questions you ask. Analyze the percentage of lower-level versus higher-level questions and see whether you are striking a good balance. Share the results with your study group, and get ideas from colleagues on puzzling issues.

Discussion Approaches

A recent review of research on classroom discussions (Wilkinson 2009) reveals high-level talk about text improves students' comprehension. This is especially true for students who are reading at or below grade level. Slavin and colleagues (2008; 2009) also found that intervention approaches that focused on talk about text were effective for elementary and secondary students. Children should be encouraged to engage in high-level thinking about what they read and to share their responses to text. They should also be encouraged to share the strategies that they used to clear up a confusing or an ambiguous passage.

Book Club, Questioning the Author, and Instructional Conversations are three discussion formats that promote high-level thinking and talk about text. I would recommend that you select one to work on with your EIR students in the spring if you feel they are ready for new challenges. Again, it's essential to meet with colleagues to share successes, ask questions, and brainstorm solutions to concerns. Every month, hold a study-group meeting to discuss issues and progress in the implementation of a particular discussion approach that fosters more high-level talk and writing about text. Share data on students' growth in using the approach to engage in higher-level talk and writing about text. Also share data on your ability to use the discussion approach effectively with students. (Figure 7–6 provides a framework for these meetings, along with additional suggestions.) Specific professional learning activities are included in the discussion of each approach.

Book Club

Book Club (McMahon et al. 1997; Raphael and McMahon 1994; Raphael et al. 2002) is a literature-based approach to reading and writing that includes peer-led discussion groups, whole-class discussions, and reading instruction. It has four components: community share, reading, writing, and small-group peer-led discussions.

Community Share

Community share consists of whole-class instructional activities and discussions about the trade books students are reading. The teacher provides explicit instruction, scaffolds students' learning, acts as a facilitator, and participates in the discussions as one of the community of readers. Students participate in instruction, share ideas and responses to books, discuss anything confusing, clarify their understanding, raise questions, generate predictions, and make connections to previously read books and to their own lives.

Reading

The reading component emphasizes constructing meaning, responding to text, and engaging in discussion. Students keep logs of their questions, ideas, reading strategies, and responses to the books they are reading. These logs are used to guide their small-group and whole-class discussions. Teachers use the logs to evaluate learning and to support subsequent instruction.

Writing

Writing is integral to this approach. Students undertake personal, creative, and critical writing. In their personal writing, students focus on valuing the book and sharing their own stories and memories. They record the feelings they had as they read, their level of enjoyment, and the experiences they've had that relate to the book. Writing creatively, students place themselves in the situation described in the story, change a story event, extend the story, write letters to the author, ask the author questions, or imagine themselves as the author. Writing critically, students analyze the literary elements, the author's message, or the effect of the story.

Small-Group Discussions

Student-led small-group discussions are the heart of the Book Club approach. During Book Club meetings, heterogeneously grouped students help one another construct meaning, analyze and synthesize information, and solve problems.

Action Steps

1. Read *Book Club: An Alternative Framework for Reading Instruction* (Raphael and McMahon 1994) or look through *Book Club: A Literature-Based Curriculum*, 2nd ed. (Raphael, Pardo, and Highfield 2002). Discuss how Book Club could be incorporated into your EIR instruction.

2. Implement Book Club for 6 weeks, 10 weeks, maybe even longer. Keep a journal of your Book Club experiences and share them with peers during study-group meetings. (Use the general plan for a series of study-group meetings described in Figure 7–6.)

Questioning the Author

In this approach you ask initiating and follow-up queries to prompt students' engagement with text (Beck et al. 1996, Beck and McKeown 2006). During discussions, students elaborate and build on one another's responses as they construct meaning together.

Initiating Queries

Questions like *What is the author trying to say here? What is the author's message? What is the author talking about?* prompt perspective and understanding. They direct attention to the main ideas and remind students that the text was produced by an author who has a point of view and who is not infallible.

Follow-Up Queries

Follow-up queries help students integrate and connect ideas. Examples include *What does the author mean here? Does the author explain this clearly? Does this make sense with what the author told us before? How does this connect to what the author told us here? Does the author tell us why? Why do you think the author tells us this now?* Special queries for narrative text are *How do things look for this character now? How has the author let you know that something has changed? How has the author settled this for us? Given what the author has already told us about this character, what do you think he is up to?*

Action Steps

1. Read "Questioning the Author" (Beck et al. 1996) or look through *Improving comprehension with Questioning the Author: A fresh and expanded view of a powerful approach* (Beck and McKeown 2006).

2. Discuss with your colleagues how Questioning the Author could be incorporated into your EIR instruction. Use the general plan for a series of study-group meetings described in Figure 7–6.

3. Try the approach in your classroom. Choose a section of content-area text for your EIR group(s) to read. Assign the role of teacher to one group member. After the students have read the text, have the "teacher" lead the discussion. Encourage students to begin with initiating queries and move on to follow-up queries. Help them build on one another's responses. Have the group discuss their experiences. Make sure the "teachers" share how they felt leading the discussion.

4. Evaluate your classroom experience with your study group. Compare this kind of discussion with the typical classroom discussion, in which the teacher initiates questions, children respond, and the teacher evaluates the responses.

Instructional Conversations

Research shows that Instructional Conversations (Goldenberg 1992; Saunders and Goldenberg 1999) enhances limited English proficient students' and fully English proficient fourth- and fifth-grade students' comprehension of stories. After reading a story, have students write about one of its themes in their literature log. Then ask them to share their entries with the group, and lead a discussion about the similarities and differences between the students' experiences and those of the main character. The following day, ask questions to clarify the events in the story and also ask higher-level questions to develop students' understanding of the theme of the story.

Action Steps

1. Read "Instructional Conversations: Promoting Comprehension Through Discussion" (Goldenberg 1992).

2. Follow the general plan for a series of study-group meetings in Figure 7–6. Discuss how Instructional Conversations could be incorporated into your EIR instruction.

3. As a study group, conduct an adult version of the activity (see Figure 4–5). Discuss the elements of having a book discussion.

4. Implement Instructional Conversations and literature logs with your EIR students. Keep reflective notes to share with colleagues in a study group.

Trying Out Literature Logs and Instructional Conversations

1. Read *The Scarebird* by Sid Fleischman (1994).

2. Talk about how you might typically discuss this story (a) during reading or (b) after reading.

3. Focus instead on a theme-based discussion. Start by writing about friendship as students might write in a literature log (describe it).

4. Discuss these questions as students might in an Instructional Conversation:

   Was Scarebird a friend to Lonesome John? Defend your position.

   Was Lonesome John mostly being nice to Sam or did he have other motives? Defend your position.

   Were Lonesome John and Sam friends at the end of the story? Defend your position.

5. Look at your description of friendship. See if there is anything you want to add to it.

6. Reflecting on your discussion of *Scarebird* or other book discussions you have had (e.g., participation in a book club), discuss elements of having/engaging in a book discussion. What will children need help with?

Figure 4–5 *Trying Out Literature Logs and Instructional Conversations*

5. Discuss your experiences with your study group. How is this approach alike or different from current practices in your school? What will children need help with?

Additional Instructional Strategies that Focus on Word Recognition

To meet your fourth and fifth grade students' individual needs in EIR, you draw from your own teaching experiences, your instincts about the child, as well as the content of the lesson procedures described in the previous chapter. In the remainder of this chapter, I highlight some additional teaching strategies for you to consider if you need to provide a child with additional support in word recognition accuracy or fluency.

One-on-One Reading with a Volunteer or Educational Assistant

For students who are struggling with word recognition, have them read their EIR nonfiction text once a week with an adult who has received training on how to coach in word recognition. This one-on-one reading should be done as early in the week as possible when the book is still a challenge to the student. By the end of the week they will have read the selection multiple times and the reading of the selection will be much easier for them; thus they will not need as much coaching support. This opportunity to read one-on-one with a coach also gives students the chance to practice decoding and reading with fluency in a relaxed environment. More discussion of one-on-one coaching and how to provide training to the adults serving in this role is in Chapter 7.

Oral Reading Analysis and Instruction

If you have students who are still struggling with word recognition, begin oral reading analysis with them (Taylor et al. 1995). You can do this on Day 3 or 5. In oral reading analysis, you take three, 100-word samples of a student's reading of material at his or her instructional level (92–97 percent accuracy in word recognition). This material should be texts read "cold," or not read before by the student. The multiple readings can be spread out over a week to ten days. You analyze these samples to determine one problem area to focus on and provide instruction. As the student does subsequent oral readings, you continue to assess in this focus area, monitoring with a progress chart to document the student's growth in the target area. Once the student has made good progress in one problem area, move to another as needed. Potential problem areas and recommendations for instruction follow. The procedures for oral reading analysis are described next in Figures 4–6 and 4–7, and a chart you can use to take notes when you conduct oral reading analysis is in Figure 4–8 and on the DVD.

Oral Reading Analysis Sample

The following is an example of a child's reading of a story, marked as an oral reading analysis. (What the student read is in parentheses; words in bold are the actual words in the text.) Note that the child has read this story with 94 percent accuracy, so it is at the appropriate level for oral reading analysis. *SC* is used to indicate a self-correction and is not counted as an error. *SD* is used to indicate a word the student had to stop on to decode, but the student was successful in coming up with the word without even making a self-correction.

> Once upon a time, a man lived in a **hut** (house) with his mother, his wife, and six children. It was very crowded and **noisy** (nosy) in the hut. So the man went to see the **wiseman** (SD). The wiseman told him to put his **chickens** (chicks), goat, and cow in the hut. The man did as he was told. Now it became very, very crowded and **noisy** (noise—noisy, SC) in the hut. The man was **exasperated** (experated), so he went back to see the wiseman. The wiseman told him to take the animals out of the hut. The man did as he was told.

Type of Error and Problem/Instruction and Ongoing Assessment

Problem	Instruction
The child doesn't know how to break a long word into chunks and blend those chunks together.	This problem is the hardest to correct. Continue to use the decoding multisyllabic words strategy discussed in Chapter 3. Model how to break a word into chunks. Coach the student to use the decoding multisyllabic words strategy himself to figure out hard words. Keep a progress chart of the number of times he at least tries to figure out hard words, or the number of times he figures out hard words.
The child makes automatic errors; that is, the word comes out almost instantly, but it is the wrong word.	At the end of the page, ask the student if she knows what word she read incorrectly. If she does not, reread the sentence the way she read it as she reads along, and ask again. Typically, when a student sees what she is doing, she begins to read more carefully and makes fewer automatic errors.
The child substitutes words that don't make sense.	At the end of a page, ask the student to identify which word in the sentence didn't make sense as he read it. If the student doesn't know, reread it for him as he read it. Have him try to figure out the correct word, paying particular attention to the meaning of the text. Keep a progress chart of the number of times the student self-corrects an error that doesn't make sense. Once this problem is brought to the student's attention, the number of self-corrections usually markedly increases.
The child misreads basic words that she knows on sight when she encounters them in isolation.	Often the student doesn't realize she is doing this. Reread the sentence (also reading the word incorrectly), and ask the child to tell you which word is incorrect. Talk about the problem of reading so quickly that one makes errors. Again, once the student sees what she is doing, she is usually able to correct this problem fairly readily.
The child skips over many or most hard words.	Often a student skips words because he doesn't know how to attack multisyllabic words. Use the suggestions in Chapter 3 to help him with this strategy. Be sure to praise a child when he does not skip over words but works at breaking them into chunks.

Figure 4–6 Oral Reading Analysis

Finally (after a pause, articulated with a short *i*), it **did** (does) not seem crowded and noisy in the hut **anymore** (SD), and the man and his family lived **happily** (happy) ever after.

Oral Reading Analysis
Sample of a Completed Recording Chart

1. Error	2. Analysis Difficulty	3. Automatic Error	4. Meaning Error	5. Other Errors (basic sight words, phonic elements, omissions)	6. Notes
hut (house)		X			
noisy (nosy)		X	X	Gave long *o* for *oi*	Told him the word to get him back on track
wiseman (SD)					
chickens (chicks)		X			
noise (noisy—SC)					
exasperated (experated)	X		X		
finally			X	After a pause, articulated with a short *i* instead of a long *i*	
did (does)		X		Basic sight word error	
anymore (SD)					Paused, then came up with the word; not counted as an error
happily (happy)		X			

Key to Columns in Chart

1. **Error.** This is an error (unless it is marked as SC or SD) due to the substitution of a real word or nonword for the actual word. The student's substitution should be written above the actual word. (SC is used to indicate a self-correction. SD is used to indicate a word the student had to stop on to decode, but the student was successful in coming up with the word without even making a self-correction. Neither of these are counted as errors when writing in a book or on a sheet.)

2. **Error Due to Analysis Difficulty.** The student does not seem to be able to work through the entire word but is only able to decode part of it. Error is marked with X in column 2.

3. **Automatic Error.** The student quickly reads the word so that it comes out automatically. However, the word is not read correctly. Error is marked with an X in column 3.

4. **Meaning Error.** The student comes up with a real word or nonword that really doesn't make sense in the context of the text being read. Error is marked with an X in column 4. Be somewhat liberal here. For example, I would not count house for hut, chicks for chickens, or happy for happily as meaning errors because I want to especially focus on instances in which the meaning is seriously impaired. (However, this involves personal judgment and I realize that some would want to count house for hut as a meaning error. I recommend that teachers try to be consistent as possible in how they score errors.)

5. **Other Errors.** Other errors are listed here, such as those in which the student gave the wrong sound for a letter or letters (wrong phonic element), the student misread a basic sight word, or the student omitted a word. For omissions, write the word in column 5 in and circle it.

6. **Notes.** In this column you can write down comments about an error or successfully decoded word or other thoughts you have about the student's reading behaviors during the oral reading.

Figure 4–7 Oral Reading Analysis

COMMENTS ON ERRORS IN SAMPLE

hut (house): Instantly came out with house and didn't self-correct.

noisy (nosy): Instantly came out with nosy, which clearly doesn't make sense in the story.

wiseman (SD): Paused, then came up with the word; not counted as an error.

chickens (chicks): Instantly came out with chicks and didn't self-correct.

noisy (noise—SC): Quickly self-corrected; not counted as an error.

exasperated (experated): Did not pronounce the second syllable; probably did not recognize, or even know, the word exasperated; should have taken a closer look at the word.

finally (after a pause, articulated with a short *i*): Not marked as a multisyllabic decoding error, since all the sounds in the word are represented; not marked as an automatic error, because he did not instantly come out with the wrong pronunciation.

happily (happy): Instantly came out with happy and didn't self-correct; not marked as a multisyllabic decoding error, since he didn't take time to break it down.

				5. Other Errors (basic sight words, phonic elements, omissions)	
1. Error	2. Analysis Difficulty	3. Automatic Error	4. Meaning Error*		6. Notes

Oral Reading Analysis Recording Sheet

Figure 4–8   Blank Oral Reading Analysis Recording Sheet

Focus for Instruction

There is no right answer about where to focus your instruction first, and you would need to look at three samples before making that decision. However, based on this one sample, because five of the child's seven errors were automatic errors, I would focus on this area first. After the child had shown improvement, I would focus on helping him correct errors that don't make sense.

Summary

Now that we have focused on instructional strategies to use with grades 4/5 students who need additional reading support, we turn to assessments. In Chapter 5, you will learn about initial assessments to determine those students who will benefit from EIR lessons, ongoing assessments to help you evaluate students' progress and make adjustments to instruction, and assessments at the end of the year to help you determine students' reading abilities as they complete fourth or fifth grade.

DISCUSS WITH YOUR COLLEAGUES

1. Discuss ways in which you could build oral reading analysis into your teaching repertoire.

2. Ask one another questions and discuss the pros and cons of teaching your students to engage in transactional strategies instruction. Share experiences with this technique.

Assessing EIR for Fourth and Fifth Graders

I n this chapter, I share fall and spring assessments that will help you deter- mine which fourth or fifth graders will benefit from supplemental reading instruction as well as provide advice for monitoring their reading progress throughout the year.

Fall Assessments

In September, assess students who appear to be reading below grade level to see whether they would benefit from supplemental EIR instruction. These assessments are typical of the kinds of classroom-based assessments teachers give their students at the beginning of the school year. If you have required assessments that give you the same information as described in this chapter, you can use them instead. All assessments are administered individually, and they are best given in the morning when children are less tired, as opposed to in the afternoon. Other children can be working on independent reading activities during this time.

Use an informal reading inventory (e.g., Qualitative Reading Inventory 4 by Leslie and Caldwell 2006) to determine which students need the grades 4/5 EIR program. Directions for administering portions of this test for the purposes of EIR placement are provided in Figure 5–1. A summarizing scoring rubric to assess comprehension (Figure 5–2) and a fall summary sheet to record scores (Figure 5–3) can also be found on the DVD.

Directions for Grades 4/5 Fall Assessment

Oral reading: Errors include substitutions, omissions, and teacher-assisted or teacher-pronounced words. Self-corrections, repetitions, proper names, or hesitations are *not* errors. If the child mispronounces the same word more than once, count each mispronunciation as an error.

Step 1. Have the student read a grade 2 or 3 passage for one minute (passage should be two grade levels below grade placement). Put a check mark above each word read incorrectly (error). If a student is stuck on a word in this 1-minute timed reading, wait about five seconds, then tell the student the word. Mark the last word read in the minute.

Step 2. Have the student continue to read the passage to the end as you mark errors made. Now that you are no longer timing the student, use your own judgment on time before telling a word, but again give about five seconds of wait time. Stop if the student is reading at less than 90 percent word recognition accuracy on the first informal reading inventory (IRI) passage (see Step 6), and do not do the summarizing or comprehension questions (continue to Steps 5 and 6).

Step 3. Ask the student to summarize the selection. Use the four-point rubric to score as shown on the Summarizing Rubric (see Figure 5–2). Record score 1, 2, 3, or 4 on the fall summary sheet (see Figure 5–3).

Step 4. Ask the student questions about the passage. Record the number and percentage of questions answered correctly on the summary sheet.

Step 5. Go back and count the number of words read correctly in one minute. Record on the summary sheet.

Step 6. Calculate word-recognition accuracy. This is the number of words read correctly (total number of words in passage minus errors) divided by the total number of words). Record on the summary sheet.

If not already done, transfer all information to Fall Summary Sheet (see Figure 5–3). If the student reads the passage that is two grade levels below grade placement with 90 percent or greater accuracy, continue to the passage that is one grade level below grade placement and repeat Steps 1–6. Stop if the child is below 90 percent accuracy and do not do the summarizing or comprehension questions (continue to Steps 5 and 6).

If the student reads the passage one grade level below grade placement with 92 percent or greater accuracy, repeat the assessment using a grade-level passage and repeat Steps 1–6. Stop if the child is below 90 percent accuracy and do not do the summarizing or comprehension questions (continue to Steps 5 and 6) and stop.

Figure 5–1 Directions for Grades 4/5 Fall Assessment

Summarizing Rubric

Passage: _____   Child's Name: _____

Summarizing: Say, "Summarize the most important ideas you just read about."

Record student's response as best as possible:

Score:

Scoring Guide:

1	2	3	4
▷ Student offers little or no information about the selection. ▷ Summary is incomprehensible. ▷ Stated ideas do not relate to the selection.	▷ Student relates details only. ▷ Student is unable to recall the gist of the selection. ▷ Summary is incomplete or ideas are misconstrued.	▷ Student relates some main ideas and some supporting details. ▷ Summary is fairly coherent.	▷ All major points and appropriate supporting details are included. ▷ High degree of completeness and coherence. ▷ Student generalizes beyond the text.

Figure 5–2 Summarizing Rubric

See the DVD for full-size versions of all the forms in this chapter.

Fall Summary Sheet

Grades 4/5	Passage two grade levels below grade placement from an informal reading inventory					Grades 4/5	Passage one grade level below grade placement from an informal reading inventory				
Student	Words Correct in First Minute	Number of Errors in Total Passage	Word-Recognition Accuracy (Percent Correct)	Summary Score (4-Point Rubric)	Questions Correct (Percent)	Student	Words Correct in First Minute	Number of Errors in Total Passage	Word-Recognition Accuracy (Percent Correct)	Summary Score (4-Point Rubric)	Questions Correct (Percent)

Grades 4/5	Grade-level passage from an informal reading inventory					Grades 4/5	Extra grade ____ passage from an informal reading inventory				
Student	Words Correct in First Minute	Number of Errors in Total Passage	Word-Recognition Accuracy (Percent Correct)	Summary Score (4-Point Rubric)	Questions Correct (Percent)	Student	Words Correct in First Minute	Number of Errors in Total Passage	Word-Recognition Accuracy (Percent Correct)	Summary Score (4-Point Rubric)	Questions Correct (Percent)

Figure 5–3 Grades 4/5 Fall Summary Sheet

Looking at Scores to See Which Children May Need EIR

In general, you are first looking for children for EIR who enter grade 4 reading on an end-of-grade-2 or beginning-of-grade-3 level or who enter grade 5 reading on an end-of-grade-3 or beginning-of-grade-4 level. If a child falls below 90 percent word-recognition accuracy on a below-grade-level passage, she most likely needs supplemental help in word recognition. If a child falls below 90 words correct per minute (wcpm) on a below-grade-level passage early in the fall, he probably needs to work on fluency. If a child can tell little about a below-grade-level or grade-level IRI passage (e.g., gets a score of 1 or 2 on the summarizing rubric) or is at the frustration level (lower than 70 percent correct) on IRI questions, she most likely needs to work on comprehension.

Providing for Children at Different Reading Levels

EIR lessons are taught to students in a group of no more than seven (which itself is a considerable challenge). If you have room in your group, children who are reading on a grade-level text with 92 percent to 97 percent accuracy in word recognition but who still have problems with fluency and/or comprehension could be included. These children may exit the EIR group before the end of the school year, and that is okay. Information to help you decide if children should exit from EIR is provided later in the chapter.

If there are more than seven children in your room who need EIR, I recommend creating two groups instead of just one. If you have a reading resource teacher at your school, perhaps she could take one group and you could take the other. With a situation like this, a number of teachers have reported switching groups periodically so they are in touch with the strengths and weaknesses of all of the EIR students in their classroom.

With two EIR groups, teachers have found that it works best to put the students who are reading at a higher level in one group and the students who are reading at a lower level in the other. In this way, the faster-moving students aren't calling out answers at the expense of the slower-moving students. Also, the slower-moving students will be less inclined to feel discouraged if they do not experience others in their group catching on more quickly.

Sometimes I am asked if a child who is reading on a beginning-of-second-grade or lower level in the fall of fourth or fifth grade should be placed in the EIR group, and my answer is, "No, unfortunately, the EIR grade 4/5 program, as designed, is too hard for them."

A child who enters fourth or fifth grade reading lower than two grade levels is in need of one-on-one support from a reading specialist. If no other supplemental instruction is available, he or she could join a grade 3 EIR group. However, it is likely that they will only be reading on an end-of-third (fourth)-grade reading level by May.

Grouping Considerations

▸ **Keep groups to no more than seven students.** Orchestrate two groups, if need be. Perhaps a reading resource teacher can take one group and you can take the other. Then, you can periodically switch groups so you have a sense of the strengths and weaknesses of all your struggling readers.

▸ **Reserve EIR instruction for teachers only.** Children at risk of reading failure desperately need quality, supplemental reading instruction from a certified teacher. Instructional aides don't have sufficient background.

▸ **Arrange two groups for optimum student participation.** If you have enough students for two groups, put the faster-progressing students in one group and the students who may need more support in the other. In this way, it won't always be the more-advanced students calling out answers at the expense of the slower-progressing students. Also, the slower-progressing students are less inclined to feel discouraged if they do not experience others in their group catching on more quickly.

▸ **Remember, children can exit from an EIR group before the end of the year.** Some students will catch up to their grade-level peers and therefore not need EIR beyond, say, February, sometimes even sooner. Guidelines to help you decide if children are ready to exit EIR are provided later in the chapter.

▸ **ELLs do well in EIR. Often, I am asked how to handle ELLs and fall placement in EIR.** Even if ELLs do relatively poorly on the fall assessment, I would put them in an EIR group in the fall unless they have the opportunity to learn to read in their first language. You do not want to take the chance of preventing any student from learning to read by postponing their participation in EIR to a later time. Also, I have found that ELLs generally do well in EIR (Taylor 2001).

▸ **Special education students do well in EIR.** I have found that EIR also works well with students who have learning disabilities. No modifications to the program are recommended.

▸ **The earlier the better.** Do not wait to place a child in EIR if he or she had low scores on all the assessments. Place them in EIR in the fall if they are reading two grade levels below grade placement or higher. If you wait to put these students in EIR in January, for example, you are likely ensuring that they will not be reading at grade level by the end of the school year.

Assessing Students' Progress in Reading During the School Year

It is always important to assess students' reading abilities and improvement in order to tailor your instruction. Therefore, opportunities are embedded within the EIR model so that teachers can monitor and document students' progress. Oral reading analysis, oral reading fluency checks, analysis of summaries, and analysis of written answers to questions are four assessments recommended when implementing EIR. (Refer back to Chapter 4 for a discussion of oral reading analysis.)

Assessing Word-Recognition Fluency: Oral Reading Fluency Check

Skilled readers are fluent readers. They are able to read orally with accuracy, automaticity (the ability to recognize a word automatically while reading), speed, proper phrasing, and expression. The benefit of fluent reading is that it enables a reader to devote maximum cognitive capacity to the meaning of the text (Kuhn and Stahl 2003; NRP 2000). Less-fluent readers focus their attention on decoding individual words and tend to read in a choppy, word-by-word manner.

One good measure of fluent reading is the number of words read correctly on a grade-level passage in one minute (wcpm score). The number of wcpm has been found to be a useful indicator of a student's reading ability, particularly for students reading on a grade 1–3 level (Fuchs et al. 2001; Kuhn and Stahl 2003). You can have them read passages from the EIR lessons and other texts at their reading level such as those read in guided reading groups. By the end of the school year, you want to see students reading at about 120 wcpm or better in grade 4 and 135 wcpm or better in grade 5.

Hasbrouck and Tindal (2006) published fall, winter, and spring oral reading norms expressed in wcpm for more than 15,000 students in first through fifth grades. The mean scores and standard deviations (in parentheses) are shown in Table 5–1.

Mean Words Correct Per Minute Scores and Standard Deviations

Grade	Mean Fall Score	Mean Winter Score	Mean Spring Score
1		23 (32)	53 (39)
2	51 (37)	72 (41)	89 (42)
3	71 (40)	92 (43)	107 (44)
4	94 (40)	112 (41)	123 (43)
5	110 (45)	127 (44)	139 (45)

Note: Standard deviations appear in parentheses.
Adapted from Hasbrouck and Tindal (2006).

Table 5–1 Mean Words Correct Per Minute Scores and Standard Deviations

Phrasing and expression while reading are also important aspects of reading fluency. In addition to assessing students' reading fluency through a wcpm score, you can use a rubric to assess student phrasing and expression while reading. The rubric developed by the National Assessment of Educational Practice (NAEP) is presented in Figure 5–4.

Assessing Students' Ability to Summarize Texts in Writing During the Year

Three or four times between the fall and spring assessments, perhaps on Day 5 of the weekly routine, have students write a summary for a reading selection that is several pages long. Use short narrative pieces or short informational texts. Use the four-point narrative summarizing rubric (Figure 5–5) or four-point informational text rubric (Figure 5–6) to score the summary. Share results with individual students and discuss with them ways they can improve their summaries in the future.

NAEP's Phrasing and Expression Scale

Level 4 Reads primarily in larger, meaningful phrase groups. Although some regressions, repetitions, and deviations from text may be present, these do not appear to detract from the overall structure of the story. Preservation of the author's syntax is consistent. Some or most of the text is read with expressive interpretation.

Level 3 Reads primarily in three- or four-word phrase groups. Some smaller groupings may be present. However, the majority of phrasing seems appropriate and preserves the syntax of the author. Little or no expressive interpretation is present.

Level 2 Reads primarily in two-word phrases with some three- or four-word groupings. Some word-by-word reading may be present. Word groupings may seem awkward and unrelated to larger context of sentence or passage.

Level 1 Reads primarily word by word. Occasional two-word or three-word phrases may occur but these are infrequent and/or they do not preserve meaningful syntax.

From http://nces.ed.gov/pubs95/web/95762.asp, U.S. Department of Education, National Center for Education Statistics

---

Figure 5–4 NAEP's Phrasing and Expression Scale

Narrative Summarizing Rubric

Directions: Ask the student to write about the most important ideas in the beginning, middle, and end of the story and what he or she thinks the author's message or theme is. Select the score that best reflects the student's summary.

1
- Student offers little or no information about the selection.
- Summary is incomprehensible.
- Stated ideas do not relate to the story.

2
- Student relates details only (details could include character, setting, some events, may not be sequential).
- Student is unable to recall many important ideas of the story from the beginning, middle, and end.
- Ideas may not be sequential.

3
- Student relates the most important ideas of the story sequentially.
- Summary is fairly coherent.

4
- Student relates the most important ideas in the story.
- Summary reflects a high degree of completeness and coherence.
- Student relates the theme or generalizes beyond the story. (The big ideas/what the author is saying to the reader.)

Example: **Scores for summaries of *The Big Orange Splot*, by Daniel Pinkwater (1993)**

1 It was about a big orange splot. The man paints at night so it can look cooler. There were lots of colors.

2 There was a big orange splot and it fell on Mr. Plumbean's house. They all made their houses like their dreams. All the people talk with Mr. Plumbean and they all talk about their favorite dreams.

3 All the people had a nice street. One day a bird comes and drops orange paint on one of the houses. The person who lives in the house goes about and gets all kind of stuff to change a house into his dreams. The other people don't like this, they want a neat street but as they go to complain, they start following their own dreams, and soon all the people in the street have followed their dreams.

4 There was a seagull and it drop a bucket of paint on Mr. P's house. So the neighbor was mad about the big orange splat on his house. So they told him to paint his house so at night he went to get paint and painted his house. The next morning the neighbors came out of their house. They said that his house is like a rainbow house. So they told Mr. P's neighbor to go tell him to paint his house the same as theirs. But whenever anybody went to Mr. P's house they end up changing their house. The author of the story is trying to tell us everything doesn't have to be the same.

Figure 5–5 Narrative Summarizing Rubric

Informational Text Summarizing Rubric

Directions: Ask the student to write about the main ideas and important supporting details contained in a page or a section of the text. Remind them that one common goal of reading informational text is to be able to use the information in the future. The summary should reflect what the author wants readers to learn from the passage. Select the score that best reflects the student's summary.

1
- Student offers little information about the selection.
- Some ideas are incomprehensible.
- Some stated ideas do not relate to the text.

2
- Student relates some details.
- Student is unable to recall most main ideas of the text.
- Summary is incomplete or ideas are misconstrued.
- Ideas may not be sequential.

3
- Student relates some main ideas and some supporting details of the text.
- Summary is sequential.
- Summary is fairly coherent.

4
- Student relates the major ideas presented in the text.
- Student includes important supporting details.
- Summary reflects a high degree of completeness and coherence.
- Student draws inferences or generalizes beyond the text.

Example: **Scores for summaries of an informational article discussing pollution and the environment**

1 Our environment was very clean but companies keep dumping waste into the lakes and rivers and the air became very dirty and nonclean.

2 It's about the environment and natural resources. And how to keep the air and water clean of wastes. And find safer things to use instead of using the harmful stuff. Most of the pollution comes from large factories that dump their wastes into rivers and harmful stuff into the air. But we've invented ways to recycle things like cans, glass, and paper.

3 There is a lot of pollution in the air and water. We should stop polluting and start using our water smarter and the same with our air. Some of our resources shouldn't be used as much because they can't be used again or there isn't that much left or they are dirty, things like coal and oil. We need to find new sources of energy such as sun and wind to help us live a lot better.

4 This article is about how to resolve pollution. Pollution can be done in water, air, and land. Water pollution makes it unfit for fish and unfit to drink. Air pollution comes from factories. Some let out poisonous gasses and make air unfit for breathing. We have not found environmentally safe ways for all of our energy needs, but people are working on it. We have found ways to recycle things which are melted and made into new things. Different new kinds of energy are solar, waterfalls, and the wind. They help us in making energy that is cleaner and won't be used up. We use energy in different ways that have different causes and effects, like pollution or not. So we should use our energy wisely. We should keep our world clean for our kids and they should do the same. (This last idea was a generalization that went beyond the text.)

Figure 5–6 Informational Text Summarizing Rubric

Assessing Students' Written Answers to Questions During the Year

Three or four times during the school year, ask students to write answers to eight or ten questions about a text they have read that is at least several pages long. Include high-level thinking questions, comprehension strategy questions, and vocabulary questions (Taylor, Garcia, and Pearson 2007). High-level thinking questions ask students to:

- Explain or interpret a story event or idea in a nonfiction selection
- Provide character interpretation (text is a narrative)
- Discuss a theme or main idea of the selection
- Relate to personal experience

Comprehension strategy questions require the use of:

- comprehension monitoring
- self-questioning
- summarizing

Examples of Questions for "Do Animals Have Feelings?"
(*Ranger Rick* Magazine, 2005)

> In a few sentences, summarize the main ideas and most important details in the article, "Do Animals Have Feelings?" (strategy: summarizing)

> What is a good question to ask other students if you want to make sure that they understood an important idea in the article? (strategy: questioning)

> Feelings create signals that other animals can recognize and understand. This can help the other animals. Give an example. (text interpretation)

> Do you think animals can show love? Why or why not? (text interpretation)

> What is the big idea that the author wants you to learn from the article? (text interpretation: main idea)

> One of your friends does not understand what it means on the second page when it says: "Some animal pairs even stay together for life. Hugging, patting, purring: These are definitely signs of bonding." How would you explain this part to your friend? (comprehension monitoring)

> Some say that animals act automatically to protect their young. What does automatically mean? (vocabulary)

> A hyena, trying to snatch food or pups from wild dogs, becomes frightened when it is outnumbered. What does *outnumbered* mean? (vocabulary)

> The article asks, "Where is the proof about animal feelings?" What does *proof* mean? (vocabulary)

RUBRIC FOR AN ANSWER TO A QUESTION

0 Off track, vague. No main idea.

1 On the right track; getting at details, may not be complete.

2 Really good; getting at bigger ideas. Gives main idea and details.

Examples of Scores for Answers to a Question on *Do Animals Have Feelings?*

A student is asked:

> What is a good question to ask other students if you want to make sure that they understood an important idea in the article?

Examples of Answers Scored as "0": Did you like the story? Did you understand the story? What do you not understand? (Score: 0—Off track)

Examples of Answers Scored as "1": What happened in the story? What was the story about? Can you summarize? Ask a question about a specific event? (Score: 1—On the right track)

Scoring Summaries and Answers to Questions as a Group

Teachers have found that they learn a great deal by scoring some of their students' summaries and answers to questions together (Taylor, Garcia, and Pearson 2007). Here is the process that a group of third-grade teachers used and their comments on the experience:

▶ Randomly select a sample of students' summaries and questions.

▶ Identify the types of questions that were asked (e.g., story interpretation/high-level thinking, comprehension strategy, vocabulary).

▶ Begin reading student responses aloud together and discuss how you would score them and record some of the student responses that fit under scores 0, 1, or 2 for questions, 1–4 for summaries, as representative (e.g., anchor) examples of each. As you are scoring, you might update or revise the scoring rubrics.

Teacher Comments

▶ *We didn't think our students would be able to write answers to these questions but we decided to give it a try. We found out they could do it. It changed our perceptions and expectations of what our students can do. We realized we needed to raise the level of our instruction because our kids needed it.*

▶ *By scoring the assessments together we started thinking about how we could improve our instruction. We started talking about asking better questions and prompting students for better responses, and we realized we needed to model high-level response and summarizing.*

▶ *After assessments in November, we all realized that we needed to focus instruction on summarizing, because our third graders weren't very good at it. We were asking our kids to summarize but never showed them how to do it. We started talking about how we would model and teach them how to summarize.*

▶ *In the beginning we were excited about the questions we would ask. Then we started to understand that high-level thinking was more than just asking a good question. We had to help students answer the questions and elaborate on their answers.*

▶ *This has been a real revelation. We realized we aren't only evaluating what the kids can do; we are also evaluating our thinking and our ideas. Our instructional focus is now on acting as facilitators and doing a lot of modeling and coaching. We have seen the progress our kids are making. And you know, we are raising our expectations for our kids all the time. It has been a really exciting process.*

Taking Children Out of EIR

Often people ask how to determine when children don't need the EIR lessons any longer because they are reading so well. In this section, I list some guidelines to help you make this decision. Some children will be ready to leave EIR lessons in January or February, but I have not found this to be too common. In general, I recommend that you be conservative and not take a child out of EIR too quickly.

Criteria for Taking a Child Out of EIR

You may decide it is time for a child to stop coming to EIR lessons because she is reading very well and the EIR lessons seem too easy. The following criteria need to be considered:

▶ The child is able to read grade-level classroom texts cold (i.e., she has not seen or read these texts before) with 95–100 percent accuracy, with good fluency (e.g., at 110–120 words correct per minute or better), and with good comprehension (90 percent correct on questions or a score of 3 or better on the four-point summarizing rubric).

▶ The child has had EIR lessons for at least two months.

▶ The child is clearly ahead of other children when working in an EIR group.

Spring Assessments

In the spring, you again need to administer an informal reading inventory to evaluate a student's reading (e.g., decoding) level, reading rate (fluency), and comprehension ability. Directions for spring assessments in fourth or fifth grade can be found in Figure 5–7. A summary sheet to record scores can be found in Figure 5–8 and a summarizing scoring rubric to assess comprehension beyond a student's ability to answer questions is provided in Figure 5–2.

Evaluating Students' Progress at the End of the School Year

▶ At the end of the school year, you need to evaluate EIR children's ability to decode an informal grade-level passage with at least 92 percent accuracy. Hopefully, your fourth- and fifth-grade children, including ELLs and students with learning disabilities, get to an end-of-fourth (or fifth) grade level. In my research 98 percent of the children in grade 4 EIR groups and 100 percent of the children in grade 5 EIR groups have been able to do so (Taylor 2001).

▶ Another factor you have to consider is the child's fluency as measured by words correct per minute. In a national study, Hasbrouck and Tindal (2006) found the average fourth grader was able to read grade 4 texts at a rate of 123 words correctly per minute, the average fifth grader was able to read grade 5 texts at a rate of 139 words correctly per minute.

▶ You should also be concerned about a child's comprehension as measured by answering passage questions and summarizing. We would like to see a child answer at least 70 percent of the questions correctly and get a summarizing score of 3 or 4.

▶ If a child falls below 92 percent word recognition accuracy on an informal reading passage that is one grade level below grade placement, he may need supplemental help in word recognition in the fall of the next school year. If in the spring a child reads fewer than 100

Directions for Spring Assessment

Oral reading: Errors include substitutions, omissions, teacher-assisted or teacher-pronounced words. Self-corrections, repetitions, uncommon proper names, or hesitations are *not* errors.

Step 1. Have student read a grade-level passage from an informal reading inventory. Put a check mark above each word read incorrectly (error). If a student is stuck on a word, wait about 5 seconds, then tell the word. Mark the last word read in the minute.

Step 2. Have the students continue reading the passage to the end as you mark the errors made. Now that you are no longer timing the student, use your own judgment on time before telling a word, but probably give about five seconds of wait time. Stop if the child is reading at less than 90 percent word-recognition accuracy (see Step 6), and do not ask the child to summarize or respond to comprehension questions (continue to Steps 5 and 6).

Step 3. Have the student summarize the selection. Use the four-point rubric to score (see Summarizing Rubric in Figure 5–2). Record scores 1, 2, 3, or 4 on Spring Summary Sheet (see Figure 5–8).

Step 4. Ask the student questions about the passage. Record the number and percentage of questions correct on the questions sheet.

Step 5. Go back and count the number of words read correctly in 1 minute. Record this number on the summary sheet.

Step 6. Go back and count the number of errors in the total passage. Calculate word-recognition accuracy. This is the number of words read correctly (total number of words in passage minus errors) divided by the total number of words. Record on the summary sheet.

If not already done, transfer all the information to Spring Summary Sheet.

If the student reads the grade-level passage with 92 percent or greater accuracy, repeat the assessment using a passage one grade level above grade placement. If the student reads the grade-level passage with below, but close to, 92 percent accuracy, repeat the assessment using a second grade-level passage. If the student is still below 90 percent accuracy on the second grade-level passage, you may wish to repeat the assessment using a passage one grade level below grade placement.

Figure 5–7 Directions for Spring Assessment

Spring Summary Sheet

Grades 4/5	Grade-level passage from an informal reading inventory					Grades 4/5	Passage one grade level above grade placement from an informal reading inventory				
Student	Words Correct in First Minute	Number of Errors in Total Passage	Word-Recognition Accuracy (Percent Correct)	Summary Score (4-Point Rubric)	Questions Correct (Percent)	Student	Words Correct in First Minute	Number of Errors in Total Passage	Word-Recognition Accuracy (Percent Correct)	Summary Score (4-Point Rubric)	Questions Correct (Percent)

Grades 4/5	Extra grade _____ passage from an informal reading inventory					Grades 4/5	Extra grade _____ passage from an informal reading inventory				
Student	Words Correct in First Minute	Number of Errors in Total Passage	Word-Recognition Accuracy (Percent Correct)	Summary Score (4-Point Rubric)	Questions Correct (Percent)	Student	Words Correct in First Minute	Number of Errors in Total Passage	Word-Recognition Accuracy (Percent Correct)	Summary Score (4-Point Rubric)	Questions Correct (Percent)

Figure 5–8 Grades 4/5 Spring Summary Sheet

wcpm in grade 4 or 120 wcpm in grade 5, he may benefit from work on fluency in the upcoming school year. If a child can tell little about a grade-level informal reading passage (a summarizing score of 1 or 2) or is reading at the frustration level on comprehension questions (lower than 70 percent correct) in the spring, he probably needs to work on comprehension in the fall.

Summary

This chapter introduced you to the assessment procedure used to support and successfully implement EIR. Watching students closely as they tackle the complex task of learning to read is imperative so that your teaching can be informed by what students know and are able to do as well as by what causes them to struggle. The multiple opportunities to assess students' reading and comprehension throughout the EIR five-day cycle and transition phase provide you with a framework that offers your struggling readers the best possible chances for success.

In the next chapter, I take a broader look at the teaching of reading once again so you will be able to dovetail what you've learned about EIR with your regular reading instruction. Specifically, Chapter 6 describes how EIR fits into a reading block and how to provide motivating, intellectually challenging independent learning activities to all of your students while you work with guided reading groups of your EIR group.

Managing Your Reading Block with EIR

In this chapter, we look at how EIR lessons fit within the reading block, reading/writing block, or literacy block. Teachers arrange their literary time in ways that suit their individual teaching styles and students' needs, and the EIR lessons are effective in many iterations of effective instruction. However, as discussed briefly in Chapter 1, some components are in place no matter what: whole-group instruction, small-group instruction (including guided reading and EIR lessons), and independent reading/learning activities for students while the teacher is with small EIR groups.

Take a look at your reading block schedule. Research shows that effective teachers *balance* whole-class and small-group instruction (Allington and Johnston 1998; Pressley et al. 2003; Taylor et al. 2007). My research also shows that too much time spent on whole-group instruction (60 percent or more) or too much time spent on small group (85 percent or more) does not have a positive impact on students' reading growth (Taylor et al. 2000; Taylor et al. 2007).

With this balance in mind, you might begin the reading block with a whole-group lesson in which you provide explicit instruction in a reading skill or strategy, using a high-quality trade book or carefully selected literature from a basal reader anthology. Teach the reading skill or strategy in the context of students' engaging with and enjoying a story or piece of nonfiction. Then you can move into small guided reading groups to differentiate instruction, including follow-up instruction on the skill or strategy covered in the whole-group lesson. You and your students should be aware of the connection among whole-group, small-group, and one-on-one instruction; it should not be a hidden thread but a visible thread. Students are in a much better position to learn when you explicitly name the connection for them. For example, in Katie Tanner's whole-group lesson detailed in Chapter 2, she teaches a 5-minute minilesson on understanding cause-effect relationships (a state-mandated skill) and tells students they will also work on cause-effect relationships in their book club groups later in the period.

Helpful Resources

Fountas, I., and G.S. Pinnell. 2001. *Guided Reading and Writing: Grades 3–6.* Portsmouth, NH: Heinemann.

Johnson, D. 2008. *Teaching Literacy in Fourth Grade.* New York: Guilford.

Lapp, D., D. Fisher, and T.D. Wolsey. 2009. *Literacy Growth for Every Child: Differentiated Small-Group Instruction, K–6.* New York: Guilford.

Lipson, M.Y. 2007. *Teaching Reading Beyond the Primary Grades.* New York: Scholastic.

Manning, M., G. Morrison, and D. Camp. 2009. *Creating the Best Literacy Block Ever.* New York: Scholastic.

McMahon, S.I., and J. Wells. 2007. *Teaching Literacy in Fifth Grade.* New York: Guilford.

Pressley, M. 2006. *Reading Instruction That Works: The Case for Balanced Teaching.* 3rd ed. New York: Guilford.

Routman, R. 2003. *Reading Essentials.* Portsmouth, NH: Heinemann.

———. 2008. *Teaching Essentials.* Portsmouth, NH: Heinemann.

Seravallo, J. 2010. *Reading Instruction in Small Groups.* Portsmouth, NH: Heinemann.

Southall, M. 2009. *Differentiated Small-Group Reading Lessons.* New York: Scholastic.

Tyner, B., and S.E. Green. 2005. *Small-Group Reading Instruction: A Differentiated Teaching Model for Intermediate Grade Readers, Grades 3–8.* Newark, DE: International Reading Association.

Effective teachers use good classroom management practices (Allington and Johnson 1998; Pressley et al. 2003). There are many excellent professional books, such as those listed in this chapter, that can help you develop and manage a dynamic literacy block, but for now, here are a few key components to implement:

- Work with students to establish classroom rules and routines to minimize disruptions and to provide smooth transitions within and between lessons.

- Use positive language and a motivating, engaging environment to impact students' behavior.

- Make a conscious effort to develop self-regulated, independent learners.

- Create a positive classroom atmosphere by demonstrating enthusiasm for learning and have high expectations for your students.

Management Ideas

Some fourth- or fifth-grade teachers I have worked with have engaged in the following practice to promote a constructive, classroom environment. Notice that teachers negotiate the criteria for behavior with students and refine it throughout the year. Some teachers generate and revise lists of expected behaviors and routines as a shared writing activity.

How to Promote Positive Classroom Environment

- Generate rules as a class during the first week of school.

- Read through classroom rules with students and talk about them at the morning meeting.

- Ask students to evaluate their actions after a discussion or activity, focusing on strengths and areas that need improvement.

- Teach students how to compliment each other and encourage them to be respectful of one another.

- Have a brief class meeting at the end of the day and ask students how well they thought their behaviors were that day, based on the rules they have generated as a class.

- Use routines and procedures to handle disruptions effectively and efficiently.

- Use routines and procedures to provide for smooth transitions within and between lessons.

- Show students that you care about them as individuals but also let them know that you will be firm, holding them to high standards as learners and good citizens.

- Give specific, constructive feedback to students regularly, provide encouragement, and challenge them to think more deeply.

Reading Block Schedules: Examples of Effective Balance

The three teachers you met in Chapter 2 typically start their reading block with a 10- to 20-minute whole-group lesson (often broken up with brief partner work) and then facilitate 15- to 20-minute small-group lessons in which they provide differentiated instruction directed toward those students' reading abilities and needs. All three teachers also provide EIR lessons to their lowest-achieving readers. The three teachers explicitly state their lesson purposes in both whole- and small-group lessons. They move at an efficient pace, guided by lesson goals, and meet with as many small groups as possible. Each teacher's schedule is included here along with a brief discussion of how the reading block might be structured.

Katie's Daily Schedule Reading Block

9:00–9:10	Whole-group minilesson
9:10–9:25	Small Group 1
9:30–10:45	Small Group 2
10:50–10:05	Small Group 3
10:10–10:30	EIR Lesson

Katie has a 90-minute reading block. She spends about 10 minutes on a whole-group lesson, 55 minutes on three guided reading groups, and 20 minutes on one EIR group (a second shot of quality instruction for her struggling readers).

Average and above-average readers spend about an hour a day on independent learning activities that include independent reading; below-average readers spend about 40 minutes a day on three separate independent learning activities, one of which may be completing follow-up work related to their EIR lesson.

Several days a week a parent volunteer listens to Katie's EIR students reread their texts and helps them with their independent activities. The volunteer also accompanies the EIR students to the third-grade classroom when they work with their third-grade buddies. Eric and Maria have 90- to 100-minute reading blocks that are similar to Katie's block. Maria works with her EIR group after lunch while the other students complete literacy work they began in the morning or read independently for pleasure.

Independent Activities

A common question that teachers ask as they begin EIR lessons with their struggling readers is, *What are my other students doing when I teach my EIR group?* In order for you to be able to spend quality time with your EIR group, you need to supply independent activities that are challenging and motivating and keep students engaged. This section includes differentiated independent literacy activities that Katie, Eric, and Maria created for their students, along with additional suggestions and resources. Hopefully, some of these ideas will be useful and will energize your teaching.

Independent Activities in Katie's, Eric's, and Maria's Classrooms

Independent activities that Katie, Eric, and Maria structure for their students include working independently, with a partner, or in a small group on reading, writing in a journal, writing on an open-response sheet, talking with others

Katie's Typical Daily Reading Block at a Glance

Whole-Group Lesson (10 minutes)	Small-Group Lessons (15 minutes for each group using texts at students' reading level)	EIR Lesson (20 minutes)	Group	Activities for Independent Work Time
Read basal selection, target comprehension strategy, teach vocabulary at point of contact, discuss high-level questions, review independent activities	Coach word-recognition strategies as needed, discuss vocabulary at point of contact, provide follow-up to comprehension strategy taught in whole group, discuss high-level questions about leveled text			
X	X		Above-Average Readers*	*Activity 1*: Reading or rereading, writing, discussing as follow-up to whole-group text
				Activity 2: Reading or rereading, writing, discussing as follow-up to small-group text
				Activity 3: Reading or rereading, writing, discussing text unrelated to whole- or small-group lesson
				Activity 4: Reading book of choice for pleasure
X	X		Average Readers*	Activity 1
				Activity 2
				Activity 3
				Activity 4
X	X		Below-Average Readers**	Activity 1
		X		Activity 2 or 3
				Activity 4

*10–20 minutes for each activity, for a total of 60 minutes

**10–20 minutes for each activity, for a total of 40 minutes

about what they have read or written about in their reading, and going on the computer to read or gather new information. What follows are some examples. You may be able to use or adapt a number of the open-ended response sheets in Figures 6–1 to 6–13 (and described later in this chapter) for these activities.

Independent Activities in Katie, Eric, and Maria's Classrooms

▶ **Complete strategy work as a follow-up to a whole- or small-group lesson:**

- With a partner, finish a topic map on a main character from a basal reader story that students started during their whole-class lesson.

- Read and summarize each page of a nonfiction article as a follow-up to a whole class lesson.

- With a partner, read and summarize remaining sections of a nonfiction text that is at a just-right reading level. Discuss confusions and talk about vocabulary during reading.

- Practice reciprocal teaching in groups of three with books of choice.

▶ **Write in reader response journals and share:**

- Respond to high-level questions the teacher has written on the board and make text-to-life connections.

- Choose one topic from the book club log list to respond to (e.g., character map, What would I do?, critique, questions to ask my group) (Raphael et al. 2004).

See the DVD for full-size versions of all the forms in this chapter.

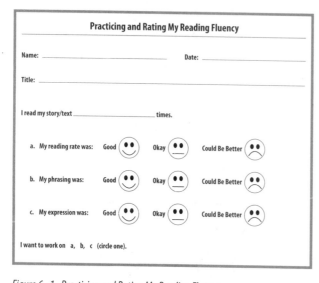

Figure 6–1 *Practicing and Rating My Reading Fluency*

Log for Independent Pleasure Reading

Name: _____ Date: _____

Book Title	Date	Start Page	End Page	My Ideas/Questions Are:

Figure 6–2 *Log for Independent Pleasure Reading*

Concept Map

Name: _____ Date: _____

Book Title: _____ Page: _____

Author: _____

It means:

My connection:

Useful word:

Sentence:

An example:

Figure 6–3   Concept Map

Cause-Effect Chart

Name: _____ Date: _____

Book Title: _____

This happened (Cause)	On page	That made this happen (Effect)	On page	My ideas

Figure 6–4   Cause-Effect Chart

Topic Map

Name: _____ Date: _____

Write words and phrases in the boxes below.

Why this topic is important:

Problem 1:

Solutions:

My topic is:

Problem 2:

Solutions:

Important concluding ideas:

Figure 6–5   Topic Map

Comparison Chart (Example)

Books: _____

Name: _____ Date: _____

	Animal 1: Wolf	Similar (S) or Different (D)	Animal 2: Coyote
Appearance	60–150 pounds, gray coloring	D, S	20–50 pounds, gray coloring
Food	Larger animals: deer, elk, bison, beavers	D, S	Smaller and some larger animals: rabbits, rodents, deer
Habitat	Forest and tundra	D	Forests, deserts, rural and urban areas
Range	Mostly Canada, Alaska, and parts of North West and North Central U.S.	D	Throughout U.S., Canada, Mexico
Interesting Facts	Travel in a pack	D	Travel alone

Figure 6–6   Comparison Chart Example

Fact-Opinion Chart

Name: _____

Book Title: _____

Author: _____

Idea (sentence)	Page	Fact (F) or Opinion (O)	Why?

Figure 6–7 Fact–Opinion Chart

Narrative Summary Sheet

Name: _____

Book Title: _____

Summarize the story in complete sentences.

Beginning (who, where, problem):	Middle (events related to problem):
End (solution):	Theme or author's message:

New Words

Write two words that you did not know or that you found interesting and what you think they mean.

Word	Page	Meaning

Figure 6–8 Narrative Summary Sheet

Summary Sheet for Informational Text

Name: _____

Summarize the informational text you read. Write in complete sentences.

	Main Idea	Important Supporting Details
PART 1		
PART 2		
PART 3		

New Words

Write two words and what they mean.

Word	Page	Meaning

Figure 6–9 Summary Sheet for Informational Text

Note-Taking Sheet on Comprehension Monitoring

Name: _____   Date: _____

Word or idea that confused me	Page	Notes

Figure 6–10 Note-Taking Sheet for Comprehension Monitoring

Note-Taking Sheet for Practicing Reciprocal Teaching Strategies

Name: _____ Book Title: _____

A. Summarizing the Text

Tell about what you read in just one or two sentences (for pages _____).

B. Generating Questions Based on the Text

Ask two important questions about what you read:

1. (from page _____)

2. (from page _____)

C. Clarifying—Check for Understanding

Note other ideas you have questions about or vocabulary you need to understand better.

1. (from page _____)

2. (from page _____)

D. Predicting

Write a prediction about what you think will be in the next section of the text (if a prediction comes to mind).

Repeat Steps A–D for the next section of the text.

Figure 6–11   Note-Taking Sheet for Practicing Reciprocal Teaching Strategies

Note-Taking Sheet for a Book Report

Name: _____ Date: _____

A. Beginning: Characters, Setting, Problem

B. Events

C. Solution to Problem

D. Author's Message

Share Your Ideas

1. Tell about a part you liked or didn't like, and why.

2. Tell how this is like your life and why.

New Words

Write two words that you did not know or that you found interesting and what you think they mean.

Word	Page	Meaning

Figure 6–12   Note-Taking Sheet for a Book Report

Note-Taking Sheet for a Book Club Discussion

Book Title: _____

People in my group:

Write two good discussion questions about the story (why, how, what do you think?).

1.

2.

Share Your Ideas

1. Tell about a part you liked and why.

2. Tell how this is like your life and why or make a connection to the world around you.

New Words

Write two words and what you think they mean.

Word	Page	Meaning

Figure 6–13   Note-Taking Sheet for a Book Club Discussion

See the DVD for full-size versions of all the forms in this chapter.

▶ **Write on index cards and share:**

• Generate questions and write down interesting or unknown words, write summaries in journals in preparation for book club.

▶ **Write on sticky notes and share:**

• Write down the meanings of unknown words from the small-group text.

• Write down dazzling words to share from independent reading.

• Use sticky notes to write summaries of pages of text, as well as ideas or vocabulary that need clarifying.

▶ **Read, write, and discuss in book clubs:**

• Read the next chapter or two in a book club book and write good discussion questions/ideas.

• Discuss chapters from a book club book, using questions generated before the club meeting.

▶ **Read, write, and share ideas from informational texts:**

• Complete a summary of a section of a National Geographic social studies or science reader at a just-right reading level.

• Write about what was interesting or surprising after reading from a National Geographic social studies or science reader at a just-right reading level.

• Select a science project topic, read about it, and write up research questions and a project plan of action to share during a science lesson.

▶ **Engage in independent reading for pleasure at just-right (independent) reading level: Keep a log.**

As we can see from the previous list, Katie, Eric, and Maria provide challenging learning activities during independent work time. They have students engage in:

▶ independent and partner work related to high-level talk and writing in response to what they are reading

▶ student-led discussions of book club books

▶ researching and writing reports based on books of their own choosing

▶ independent reading for pleasure from books of their own choosing for about 20 to 30 minutes

It is important to remember to watch students closely to see if the independent work is both motivating and challenging. Choice is also important. When students are given the opportunity to choose how to respond to the books they've read, they become more engaged in the process and this choice fosters independence and responsibility.

More Suggestions for Challenging Independent Activities

Independent work time can be one of the most academically powerful junctures of the school day, because it is when students actually practice being independent readers. Making independent time work well is crucial because, after all, one of our goals is to create self-regulated and motivated learners.

What factors prevent students from learning to read and learning to enjoy reading? Low-level tasks are one major factor. Research by Pressley at al. (2003) has found that teaching behaviors that undermined academic motivation included assigning activities in which students were asked to complete tasks that were too easy, required low cognitive effort, and demanded little of them.

In my many visits to fourth- and fifth-grade classrooms over the ten years I worked with schools on schoolwide reading improvement (Taylor et al. 2005; Taylor 2010c), I often saw students engaged in primarily low-level tasks during independent work time. Typically, these students were reading or rereading basal selections or guided reading group books and answering low-level questions, completing worksheets or workbook pages, working on spelling or grammar, and engaging in independent reading with no follow-up or accountability required. Also, these activities could often be completed in much less time than what was allowed, which only compounded the likelihood that students dawdled, got off task, chatted with students near them, or wandered around the room.

At the other end of the spectrum, during my school visits, I also visited exciting classrooms in which students were participating in many tasks requiring high-level thinking and collaboration during independent work time. The levels of student engagement and the number of happy faces and excited eyes in these classrooms as compared to classrooms with less motivating activities were striking. Students typically had three or four activities to complete that kept them meaningfully engaged and working at a continuous, efficient pace. With enough to do and with interesting things to work on, students did not get off task. Most important, they appeared to be happy learners.

These observations are supported by the research of Allington and Johnston (1998) on tasks that facilitate academic motivation in fourth-grade classrooms. They found that teachers motivated learners when they engaged them in cooperative learning and high-order, critical, and creative thinking. For example, fourth graders might discuss a book in a student-led book club after having first responded in writing to a number of high-level questions, or two students might research a social studies or science topic related to state or district standards and collaboratively write (or co-present) a report. Motivational teachers also used engaging and interesting texts that aroused students' curiosity, got them excited about their learning, and exposed them to high-quality literature.

Examples of independent work time activities that will engage students and advance their literacy abilities are provided in the next section. Independent response sheets that go with some of these suggestions are also provided.

For a discussion of word study for intermediate and advanced readers, see *Words Their Way* by Bear, Invernizzi, Templeton, and Johnston (2007).

For additional suggestions see *Bringing Words to Life: Robust Vocabulary Instruction* by Beck, McKeown, and Kucan (2002).

For additional suggestions on fluency, see *The Fluent Reader: Oral Reading Strategies for Building Word Recognition, Fluency, and Comprehension* by Rasinski (2003).

Activities That Support Word Recognition and Vocabulary Development

▶ To reinforce students' knowledge of morphology that you have recently taught in whole-group or guided reading groups, have them complete word sorts with a partner. For example, if you have recently focused students' attention on particular roots, prefixes, and suffixes, have them sort words containing these roots, prefixes, and suffixes. Have students read the words that have been sorted.

▶ If your school's spelling curriculum uses weekly spelling lists and tests, have students practice spelling misspelled words from their weekly spelling lists after you have given students a pretest and they have self-corrected misspelled words. Word lists should be differentiated based on students' reading and spelling abilities.

▶ On sticky notes or in a vocabulary journal, have students write down interesting, unknown, or newly learned words that come from the books they are reading. Students can share words and possible meanings with either the teacher in whole- or small-group lessons or by turning a vocabulary journal in to the teacher, or with a volunteer, educational assistant, or older classroom helper.

▶ Have students complete concept maps or webs for high-utility words identified by their teacher from the books they are reading.

Activities That Support Fluency

▶ With a partner, have EIR students reread stories from their guided reading group or EIR lesson. Students should coach one another on difficult words. Refer back to Chapter 3 for prompts for students to use during partner reading.

▶ Have EIR students reread stories from their guided reading group or EIR lesson with a volunteer, educational assistant, or older student helper (who coaches as students get stuck on words they cannot decode instantly).

▶ Have students reread stories and informational texts in their book box. They should list books read for fluency and self-rate their fluency on books read (see Figure 6–1).

▶ Have students read new books for pleasure. They should log books they read (see Figure 6–2).

Activities That Support Comprehension: Skills and Strategies

▶ Have students read books to practice comprehension skills and strategies. Examples of open-ended response sheets include the following: concept map (Figure 6–3), cause-effect chart (Figure 6–4), topic map (see Figure 6–5), comparison chart (Figure 6–6), fact/opinion chart (Figure 6–7), summary sheet for narrative text (Figure 6–8), summary sheet for informational text (Figure 6–9), comprehension monitoring sheet (Figure 6–10), reciprocal teaching sheet (Figure 6–11).

▶ Have students write questions as they read or after they are finished reading. Question types include: clarifying, main idea, summary, interpretive, evaluative/critical literacy.

Activities That Support Comprehension: Learning New Information

Have students engage in the following:

- Read books to learn new information about topics of interest.

- Search and read on the Internet to learn more information.

- Read books, magazines, and other texts that address grades 4/5 social studies and science topics. Teachers, the media specialist, or volunteers could locate existing books at the school or purchase books (with school funds or funds from the PTA or local businesses) at various reading levels that cover topics in social studies and science grade-level curriculum.

- Prepare and give an oral or written presentation with a partner, triad, or independently (see Figure 6–12).

- Prepare a written report. Students could do reports with a partner, triad, or independently. (See Figure 6–5 as a way to organize ideas.) Other topics for writing after reading include: procedures, recounting an event, explanation, persuasion.

- From independent reading on topics of interest, write down words to share (vocabulary) and write about them (Figure 6–3).

Activities That Support Comprehension: Talk and Writing About Text

After the teacher has modeled and done coaching lessons, students can:

- Participate in literature circles: learn routines, read, take notes, and share (Figure 6–13).

- Respond to literature (Figures 6–12 and 6–13).

- Prepare and give a book report (Figure 6–12).

- Engage in critical literacy, in which students evaluate, express, discuss, and/or write ideas related to an issue they have read about (Heffernan 2004).

For more suggestions, see:

Reading and Writing with Understanding: Comprehension in Grades 4 and 5 by Hampton and Resnick (2008).

Reciprocal Teaching at Work: Strategies for Improving Reading Comprehension by Oczkus (2003).

QAR Now by Raphael, Highfield, and Au (2006).

For more suggestions, see:

Teaching Reading Beyond the Primary Grades by Lipson (2007).

Integrating Instruction: Literacy and Science by McKee and Ogle (2005).

Concept-Oriented Reading Instruction: Engaging Classrooms, Lifelong Learning by Swan (2003).

For more suggestions, see:

Moving Forward with Literature Circles by Day et al. (2002).

Critical Literacy and Writer's Workshop: Bringing Purpose and Passion to Student Writing by Heffernan (2004).

Using Literature to Enhance Content Area Instruction: A Guide for K–5 Teachers by Olness (2007).

Comprehension Shouldn't Be Silent by Kelley and Clausen-Grace (2007).

Book Club: A Literature-Based Curriculum, 2d ed. (Raphael et al. 2002)

For more suggestions, see *Literature and the Child,* 7th ed. by Galda, Cullinan, and Sipe (2009).

Activities That Support Reading for Pleasure

Have students:

▶ Read books from different genres for 20 to 30 minutes a day. After reading, have students complete a reading log (Figure 6–2).

▶ Read different books from a favorite author.

▶ Share favorite books in a book sharing club.

▶ Write about favorite books on cards kept in a classroom file or in a folder on the computer that everyone in the class can look through for suggestions for books to read.

Independent work time is an important component of a teacher's overall classroom reading program. Students spend a considerable amount of time working on their own or with others while teachers work with small, guided reading groups. It is crucial that students are actively engaged in interesting, challenging learning activities that meet their needs and move them forward in literacy abilities during this independent work time. However, it is easy for these independent learning activities to become routine, undifferentiated, unchallenging, unnecessary practice, and not motivating or challenging to students. When this happens, it is easy for students to get off task or spend much more time than is needed on assigned activities. To alleviate these issues, many teachers find that changing the independent activities every so often works well, as does providing students with choice. Additionally, providing students with long-term projects (e.g., author studies, research projects) can also avert some of the routinization of the activities. Finally, never underestimate the power of sharing ideas with colleagues about effective independent learning activities.

For more on effective, motivating reading instruction and assessment in general:

Teaching Reading Beyond the Primary Grades by Lipson (2007).

Classroom Reading Assessment: Making Sense of What Students Know and Do by Paratore and McCormick (2007).

Reading Instruction That Works: The Case for Balanced Teaching, 3d ed., by Pressley (2006).

For more information on differentiated reading instruction and work with struggling readers, see:

Success with Struggling Readers: The Benchmark School Approach by Gaskins (2005).

After Early Intervention, Then What? Teaching Struggling Readers in Grades Three and Beyond by McCormick and Paratore (2005).

Differentiated Small-Group Reading Lessons by Southall (2009).

Creating an EIR Community

Early Intervention in Reading is a powerful approach for accelerating the reading development of children who find learning to read difficult, and in some respects it is easy to implement. The predictable structure, small-group attention, the motivating literature at its heart make it something that teachers and children quickly grow to like. However, because it isn't a curriculum but rather a repertoire of teaching strategies, and because any learner who struggles requires teachers to reflect and use considerable skill, I strongly encourage teachers to enlist support along the following three lines:

1. Teachers need to work with colleagues during their first year of teaching EIR lessons.

First and foremost, over many years, I have found that teachers experience more success with their students when they regularly participate in monthly meetings with colleagues to discuss EIR during the first year they are teaching the lessons. Together, teachers can clarify procedures, share successes, and help one another solve problems. Teaching EIR lessons for students who need more support along with effective whole-group and small-group instruction amounts to highly differentiated teaching for all students—not an easy thing to achieve.

In a research study on effective reading practices (Taylor et al. 2000), the most effective schools had a collaborative model for delivering reading instruction in which struggling readers received a second, 30-minute small-group reading intervention each day to accelerate their literacy learning. Therefore, I strongly recommend that classroom teachers, Title 1 and other reading resource teachers, ELL teachers, and special education teachers who work together meet as a group in monthly EIR professional learning experiences. Also, I want to stress that classroom teachers can provide the EIR instruction, or at least share the teaching of EIR lessons with a resource teacher. I developed this model with classroom teachers in mind—in other words, with the notion that classroom teachers can learn to provide additional effective instruction to students who need more reading support during the literacy block.

2. Teachers need to get help from others on scheduling the monthly meetings and sustaining the one-on-one coaching sessions that are an essential piece of EIR.

If numerous teachers are learning about and teaching EIR in the same year, it is extremely helpful if a school has a building facilitator to provide support. This person can take responsibility for securing EIR books and materials; for scheduling professional learning sessions, such as those described below; for establishing the one-on-one word recognition coaching component of EIR by aides or volunteers for students who need support (as discussed in Chapter 4 and later in this chapter); and for problem-solving as issues arise.

3. Teachers need to do outreach to parents/caregivers, so that these adults can help their children practice reading at home.

Parents have a critical role to play in EIR. Children take their EIR story home at the end of the third day so they can read to their parents or tell them about their book and get ready for their cross-age tutoring with a younger student, or EIR partner, as described in Chapter 3. In Figure 7–1, there is an Individual Take-Home sheet for parents to sign. Parents should sign the EIR take-home sheets and have their children bring them back to school.

To introduce EIR activities to parents, a sample letter you can send home explaining the program is shown in Figure 7–2. Also, at the beginning of the school year, you can invite parents and students to an EIR Information Night, perhaps at the school's back-to-school-night event, during which you explain the materials that will be coming home and the importance of parents'/caregivers' involvement in these activities. You can demonstrate the coaching prompts for parents at this time. Also, you may want to show parents a video of yourself coaching children in their EIR group.

For parents who can't make it to school, you can send home a video of yourself reading with their child and coaching as the child is stuck on difficult words. One teacher reported taping each child in November and May and then giving the tape to the parents at the end of the year. Another strategy teachers have used for involving parents is inviting them to school to see EIR lessons in action.

Individual Take-Home Sheet

Book Title: _____

Name: _____ **Date:** _____

Parent or Guardian Signature: _____

Reading for Fluency

I practiced reading this informational text _____ times.

_____ I am ready to read it to my younger reading buddy (or EIR partner).

_____ I need to practice some more.

Discussion

Write down one question so you and your younger reading buddy (or EIR partner) can talk about this text.

New Words

Write down two words to ask or tell your younger reading buddy (or EIR partner) and about what they mean.

  Word 1

  Word 2

See the DVD for full-size versions of all the forms in this chapter.

Figure 7–1 Individual Take-Home Sheet

Parent/Caregiver Information Letter

Dear Parent/Caregiver,

To help maximize your child's success in reading, we are using supplementary reading lessons called Early Intervention in Reading (EIR). EIR will help your child by using a different approach to experience reading success. We are excited about it!

We want to emphasize that we really need your involvement. How can you help? Watch for a book and/or take-home activities your child will bring home. Be sure to ask your child to tell you about their nonfiction text and supervise him or her with the take-home activities. Return the take-home activity with your signature. Research shows, *"Kids who read the most, read the best!"*

This is the way we teach EIR:

▶ The teacher guides students to use reading strategies as they read an informational text at their reading level in the small group or with partners.

▶ The teacher and students talk about the text, learn new words, and prepare to read and teach the text to a younger student or EIR partner. Children write about the text, based on activities the teacher has provided.

▶ The children practice reading the text at home, and come up with a good question to ask their younger reading buddy or EIR partner and two vocabulary words to teach to their younger reading buddy or discuss with their EIR partner whom they will work with one day a week. If they are working with a younger child, they will also listen to this child read and coach him or her if they get stuck on words in their grade-level text.

Remember: Ask your child to tell you about their book and assist with the take-home activities as needed. Your child will return the completed take-home activities page with your signature.

Thank you for your continued support as we work together to help your child have success in reading.

Sincerely,

Figure 7–2 Parent/Caregiver Information Letter

Overview of Monthly EIR Meetings

Now let's look at a yearly framework for professional learning sessions that includes how often to have meetings, sample agendas, and suggestions for what to address throughout the year. If you would like to receive extra support from an EIR consultant, go to www.earlyinterventioninreading.com.

At monthly meetings of about an hour, teachers learning to teach EIR lessons can work together to gain expertise and confidence about doing these intervention lessons, hone their abilities to coach children to use word-recognition strategies and depend on themselves, pose questions about the EIR texts, and coach in the use of comprehension strategies that lead to high-level, comprehension-building responses. Swapping successes, trials, classroom management ideas, and authentic independent activities—teachers can support one another around so many teaching issues.

Begin the meetings in August or September and continue through May. If it's hard to find an hour once a month, you can meet for shorter times over several days during the month. In the first 10 or 15 minutes, the group can focus on sharing ideas and concerns related to EIR lessons. Teachers can also take about 30 or 40 minutes to review and discuss grade-level procedures and the video clips of effective practice found on the DVD. By November, I encourage teachers to bring in video segments of their own teaching of EIR lessons.

August

In August, read and discuss Chapters 1 and 2 with the group of teachers in your school who are participating in the EIR professional learning sessions. You may also want to read and discuss Chapter 6, which covers fitting EIR into your daily literacy instruction and making sure your independent learning activities are challenging, motivating, and engaging so you can focus your attention on the students in your guided reading groups or EIR lessons.

September

Additionally, in August or early September, you should begin to review the EIR procedures in Chapter 3. During the September and October meetings, go through the five-day EIR routines in detail. Also, during monthly meetings, you can revisit aspects of the EIR procedures as questions arise.

October

Sometimes teachers report uneasiness about "doing the EIR procedures correctly" and want to delay getting started. However, I always tell teachers not to worry if they are doing things "just right" at first; they will get better at using EIR strategies over time. What is important is to get started with EIR lessons as close to October 1 as possible. Most children who will benefit from EIR need the intervention all year. Students should have the opportunity to be a part of reading intervention lessons that make them feel successful as soon as possible before feelings of discouragement about reading set in.

Monthly Meetings Overview

August/September	Discuss Chapters 1, 2, and 3 Watch videos Review fall assessments Prepare for October meeting
October	Status report on EIR teaching and review procedures as questions arise Review video-sharing procedures Discuss one-on-one coaching for students who need this Prepare for November meeting
November	Status report on EIR teaching and review daily procedures Status report of one-on-one coaching Video sharing/sharing Prepare for December meeting
December	One-on-one coaching status report Status report on EIR teaching: Coaching for comprehension Group activity: Book lesson share Discuss grade-level procedures Video sharing Prepare for January meeting
January	Status report on EIR teaching Discuss coaching for comprehension Discuss grade-level procedures: Oral reading analysis, reciprocal teaching as an independent study strategy Video viewing/sharing Prepare for February meeting
February	Status of children's progress Additional comprehension instruction (see Chapter 4): Reciprocal teaching as an independent study strategy, transactional strategies instruction, high level talk about text/ discussion techniques. Group activity: Discuss oral reading analysis Video sharing Prepare for March meeting
March	Status of children's progress Additional comprehension instruction: Transactional strategies instruction or high level talk about text/discussion techniques Video sharing Prepare for April meeting
April	Status of children's progress Additional comprehension instruction: Transactional strategies instruction or high level talk about text/discussion techniques Review spring assessment procedures Discuss EIR plans for next year
May (if time permits, or at a grade-level meeting)	Discuss results of assessments Status of children's progress Continue to discuss EIR plans for next year

Figure 7–3 *Monthly Meetings Overview*

November–May

Beginning in November, I recommend you incorporate video sharing into your monthly EIR meetings. To do this, teachers take turns bringing in a 5- to 8-minute video clip of their EIR teaching to share and discuss. These video-sharing experiences give teachers the opportunity to reflect on and discuss their practice. So often, professional development focuses on curriculum lessons tied to a teacher's manual or the proper use of new materials. Teachers are rarely given the opportunity, with the help of colleagues, to think, talk about, and enhance their own teaching practices.

The focus of the video sharing should be:

▶ What the children are doing well or the strengths they are demonstrating in the EIR lesson.

▶ What the teacher is doing well to foster strategy use, independence, and success in the children.

▶ What else the teacher might have done to foster strategy use, independence, and success.

Through EIR ongoing professional learning sessions, you will improve your coaching abilities. As you focus on coaching and work at it collaboratively, you will be reminded that coaching children to become independent is not easy. However, you also learn that coaching is something you can master, with the end result of having more children in your classrooms reading well by the end of the school year. Video-sharing procedures are described in greater detail in Figure 7–4 on page 107.

Recommended agendas for the year are detailed on the following pages. I suggest you read through them now as a way to get an idea of what a year of EIR professional learning might look like. Then, use the monthly agenda pages to organize and advance your EIR work and learning.

Agendas for Monthly Meetings

In the following section, a detailed yearly framework is presented for monthly meetings, including aspects of the EIR you might focus on during certain months, a structure for sharing and discussing progress and concerns, as well as protocols for viewing and sharing videos.

September Meeting (70–75 min.)

Recommended activities for professional learning in September include the following.

Review Chapters 1, 2, and 3 (10–15 min.)

Prior to the meeting, read Chapters 1, 2, 3, and 6. At the meeting talk about any remaining questions or issues you have related to Chapters 1 and 2. You may also wish to discuss Chapter 6, which covers fitting EIR into your daily instruction and offers ideas for productive independent work for other students while you are working with your EIR group.

Discuss Instructional Procedures in Chapter 3 (35–40 min.)

Carefully work through Chapter 3 and the grades 4/5 EIR routines. Also, watch the related video clips on the DVD.

Review Assessment Procedures in Chapter 5 (20 min.)

Review the fall assessment procedures described in Chapter 5. Select passages from an informal reading inventory that you will all use in the fall assessments to determine which students need EIR lessons.

Prepare for October Meeting (5 min.)

Briefly review what needs to be done before the October meeting:

▶ Identify your EIR students. Don't worry if you aren't sure about your placement decisions. You can ask questions at the October meeting and make changes then.

▶ Start your EIR lessons before you meet in October and as close to October 1 as possible. You will get more out of the October meeting if you have already started to teach EIR lessons. You should jot down notes on this instruction so you have a chance to share experiences and have your questions answered at the October meeting.

October Meeting (65–70 min.)

This month you will continue to learn and talk about instructional procedures. Additionally, you need to prepare for video sharing, which should begin in November. You also need to make sure the one-on-one reading coaching will be in place soon, if it's not already, for those few students who need additional support in word recognition.

Status Report on EIR Teaching (10 min.)

Take turns reporting on how things have gone so far with the initial teaching of EIR lessons.

Review Video-Sharing Procedures (20 min.)

Each person should bring one video to share in November, December, or January and a second in February, March, or April. Share one or two videos each month. To learn about video sharing, see Figure 7–4. (A suggested sign-up sheet is provided in Figure 7–5.)

The basic approach to video sharing was developed for the EIR Professional Development Program but has also been used successfully in other teacher professional development venues (Taylor 2011; Taylor et al. 2005). Each video-sharing segment should take no more than 15 minutes. Focus on students' strategy use, independence, and success.

Prior to coming to your study group meeting, do the following:

1. Videotape the lesson segment you selected. It should be about 5 minutes long.

2. Answer the following three video-sharing questions based on your video:

   - What things were the children able to do related to your focus area? What things were going well?

   - What was the teacher doing to help children develop and be successful related to your focus area?

   - What else could you have done to foster development and success related to your focus area?

When you share the video at an EIR session, do the following:

1. Share 1 minute of background about the lesson.

2. Tell the group an aspect of your instruction you would like their help with.

3. View the video with the group.

4. Have members break into groups of three to review the three video-sharing questions. Individuals should take notes on things the children did well, things the teacher in the clip did well in getting children to develop and succeed related to the focus area, and suggestions for things that might have been done differently to help the children develop and succeed related to the focus area.

5. Discuss the video clip as a larger group. The person serving as facilitator will ask the three video-sharing questions to the group. Members from the groups of three can share points

that they wish to share. Notes from small groups should be given to the teacher who brought the video clip of her teaching.

- The teacher who brought the clip should ask for their ideas related to item 2.

Remember, this is first and foremost a learning activity in which colleagues are helping one another improve their abilities as coaches.

At an EIR session, sign up for a topic—one part of one day's lesson.

 tip

People should sign up for the video sharing in October (see Figure 7–5). If you have more than six teachers in your group, break into groups of three to five members for the video sharing part of the meeting. With six members in a video-sharing group, you would watch two videos a month. With three members in a video-sharing group, you would watch one video a month. Everyone should share their first video in November, December, or January, and a second video in February, March, or April.

Engaging in Video Sharing

The basic approach to video sharing was developed for the EIR Professional Development Program but has also been used effectively in other teacher professional development venues. Each video-sharing segment should take no more than 15 minutes. Focus on students' strategy use, independence, and success.

Prior to coming to your study group, do the following:

a. Videotape the lesson segment you selected. It should be about 5 minutes long.

b. Answer the following three video-sharing questions based on your video:

▶ What were the things the children were able to do related to your focus area? What things were going well?

▶ What was the teacher doing to help children develop and be successful related to your focus area?

▶ What else could have been done to foster development and success related to your focus area?

When you share the video at an EIR study session, do the following:

1. Share 1 minute of background about the lesson.

2. Tell the group an aspect of your instruction you would like their help with.

3. View the video with the group.

4. Break members into groups of three to review the three video-sharing questions. Individuals take notes on things the children did well, things the teacher did well in getting children to develop and experience success related to the focus area, and offer suggestions for things you might have been done differently to help the children develop and experience success related to the focus area.

5. Discuss the video clip as a larger group. The person serving as facilitator will ask the three video-sharing questions to the group. Members from the groups of three can share points that they wish to share. Notes from small groups should be given to the teacher who brought the video clip of her teaching.

6. The teacher who brought the clip should ask for their ideas related to item 2.

Remember, this is first and foremost a learning activity in which colleagues help one another improve their skills as coaches. At an EIR session, sign up for a topic—one part of one day's lesson.

Figure 7–4 Engaging in Video Sharing

Video Sharing—Sign-Up Sheet for Grades 4/5

Month	Teacher	Description of Video
November		Teacher models and coaches on decoding strategies for multi-syllabic words as students read book on Day 1
		Coaching for comprehension
		Reciprocal teaching
December		Teacher coaches as children read story on Day 2 or Day 3
		Reciprocal teaching
		Cross-age tutoring or partner coaching session
January		Coaching for comprehension
		Debriefing on Day 5
		Reciprocal teaching
February		Oral reading analysis
		Cross-age tutoring session or partner coaching session
		Reciprocal teaching—students working independently
March		Transactional strategies instruction
		High level talk about text or discussion technique
		Working with students on grade-level text (word recognition, vocabulary, comprehension)
April		Transactional strategies instruction
		Working with students on grade-level text (word recognition, vocabulary, comprehension)
		High level talk about text or discussion technique

Figure 7–5 Video Sharing — Sign-up Sheet for Grades 4/5

One-on-One Coaching (10 min.)

Discuss the status of the one-on-one coaching piece of EIR or the plans for getting this component into place as soon as possible. Remember, this piece is only needed for those students in your group who are having difficulties with decoding. One-on-one coaches might be educational assistants, classroom volunteers, or older students who are classroom helpers who have received training on how to be a coach. (See the section on training coaches later in this chapter.)

To get maximum results with EIR for students who need additional support in word recognition, one-on-one coaching needs to occur on a regular basis. Children need the opportunity to practice reading with no other child next to them calling out words they don't know. Also, individual children need the chance to prove to themselves what they are able to do on their own. Even if you are not responsible for training one-on-one coaches, you should look through the information presented on this topic so you understand the training the coaches have received. Also, as the classroom teacher, you need to supervise the one-on-one coaches and give constructive feedback as needed.

You may find it helpful to consider the following observations I have about EIR lessons and students in October.

▶ In the fall of fourth or fifth grade, many of the children in EIR still need to work on their reading fluency. They can decode, but they are very slow. They also need to develop confidence in how to attack multisyllabic words. Review the strategy for attacking multisyllabic words in Chapter 3. This needs to be tied to the advanced vowel chart. I also find it helpful to keep stressing that this strategy will only get them close to the real word. They need to be thinking of a word that will make sense in the story as they are trying to sound out a word. Review and discuss Video 2.

▶ As children get ready to tutor, you need to discuss strategies with them for working with their younger student. They need to understand how to coach their buddy to come up with a word, not just tell the child what it is. At the same time, many of them often come up with strategies that are too advanced, such as the multisyllabic strategy they are working on for themselves. Refer back to Figure 3–9 for prompts they can use for partner reading. Also, be sure to have the fourth- and fifth-grade children practice the lower-grade story before they work with the younger students. I often find they have trouble reading the lower-grade story without practicing it first. Review and discuss Videos 6 and 7.

▶ Continue to model the four reciprocal teaching steps and coach students as they try to apply them. Good goals for October are getting students used to the idea of monitoring comprehension and having them practice the reciprocal teaching steps by analyzing text paragraph by paragraph.

Review of EIR Procedures (20–25 min.)

Refer to your notes about your EIR lessons and raise any questions you have; other members in your group may have the answers. You can also return to the section in Chapter 3 on grade-level routines to answer questions.

Preparation for November Meeting (5 min.)

For the November meeting, one or two people should bring in short video clips to share of predetermined segments of EIR lessons. (See the sign-up sheet in Figure 7–4.) An example of a segment would be steps from Days 1, 2, 3, 4, 5.

November Meeting (60–75 min.)

Status Report on EIR Teaching (10 min.)

Share successes and questions you have about EIR teaching.

One-on-One Coaching, Status Report (5 min.)

Discuss how this is working for students who need additional coaching in word recognition. Discuss any scheduling issues or concerns.

Questions About the Video Sharing (5 min.)

Discuss any questions or concerns about video sharing, logistics, and feelings you may have had about the video taping.

Discussion of Grade-Level Procedures (20 min.)

▶ By November I recommend that you work with a page of text at a time, instead of just a paragraph, as you are practicing the reciprocal teaching model. Also, if you are not already doing so, you want to be moving toward the goal of only spending 3 days on a lesson and getting through all parts of a lesson before the children tutor. Discuss strategies for getting through all parts of a lesson.

▶ If there are parts of the EIR routine that you wish to review, return to the relevant sections of Chapter 3 and the corresponding video clips.

▶ It is important to remember to have a debriefing session for your children after they work with their younger buddy or their EIR partner. Begin with sharing things that are going well and then turn to problems that need to be solved. Discuss what topics are being raised by students in these sessions.

▶ Discuss the activities you have tried for Step 2 of Day 5 (or for Days 4 and 5 if your students are not engaged in cross-age tutoring). Remember, choices include having students bring their basal reader or social studies book to EIR so you can work on attacking multisyllabic words, vocabulary, and comprehension; letting children read independently from books of their own choosing while you coach them on word recognition and comprehension or conduct an oral reading analysis or oral reading fluency check; having students write summaries or answers to text so you can assess their abilities and growth on these comprehension tasks.

Video Sharing (15–30 min.)

Preparation for December Meeting (5 min.)

For the December meeting, one or two people (depending on the size of your group) should bring in short video clips to share predetermined segments of EIR lessons.

tip

Many teachers are nervous about the video sharing, but they find it gets a lot easier by the second time. In May, on EIR evaluations, many teachers state that the video sharing was one of the most valuable parts of these EIR professional learning sessions. So hang in there with the video-sharing experience!

December Meeting (65–80 min.)

Status Report on One-on-One Coaching (5 min.)

It is very important that this component of EIR be up and running for those students who need additional support in word recognition. If possible, try to observe your one-on-one coaches so you can give them feedback.

Status Report on EIR Teaching (10 min.)

By December, the EIR procedure should seem like second nature. Therefore, it is a good time to reflect on your coaching for comprehension. Keep a list of the questions you ask your students, jot down notes on your questioning practices, and bring them to share at the January meeting.

The following are some questions to get you thinking about your questioning and coaching for comprehension:

▶ Are you asking follow-up questions to get a child to clarify what they are saying or elaborate on their ideas?

▶ Are you giving a child enough wait time?

▶ Are you coaching quiet children (e.g., those who like to say, "I don't know") to talk instead of just moving on to another child?

▶ Are you asking questions that are based on a concept in the story but that relate to children's lives?

▶ Are your questions thought provoking and meaningful to the children?

Group Activity (10 min.)

Using the books you will be using in future EIR lessons, with a partner, generate good coaching for comprehension questions. Share these with the larger group.

Discussion of Grade-Level Procedures (15 min.)

▶ By now you should be doing less modeling and more coaching as children apply the reciprocal teaching steps to their EIR texts. They will still need a fair amount of help generating important questions and summarizing sections of text in one or two sentences. Remind them to think about the "big picture" ideas the author is trying to tell them.

▶ Remind your students that as they read it is normal to encounter things that need clarification. Monitoring comprehension is a very difficult skill for some struggling readers to grasp. First they have to notice that something doesn't make sense. Then they need to know what to do about it. Continue to talk about fix-up strategies.

▶ *Group activity*: Discuss children's strengths and weaknesses in using the various parts of the reciprocal teaching model. Brainstorm ways to help them with the problems they are having.

Video Sharing (15–30 min.)

Engage in video sharing.

Preparation for January Meeting (2 min.)

For the January meeting, one or two people per group should bring in short video clips to share a predetermined piece of an EIR lesson. Remember to bring in the notes from your coaching for comprehension.

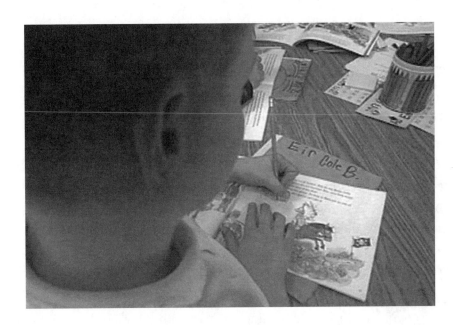

January Meeting (70–75 min.)

Status Report on EIR Teaching (5–10 min.)

Briefly report on successes you are seeing with your students—even after the holiday break!

Coaching for Comprehension (10 min.)

At the December meeting, questions were presented to help you focus on your questioning and coaching for comprehension. Discuss your notes and anything you learned about your practice from having focused on these questions.

▶ Are you asking follow-up questions to get a child to clarify what they are saying or elaborate on their ideas?

▶ Are you giving a child enough wait time?

▶ Are you working with quiet children who like to say "I don't know," instead of just moving on to another child?

▶ Are you asking questions that are based on a concept in the story or informational piece but that leave the story behind and relate to children's lives?

▶ Are your questions thought provoking and meaningful to the children?

One-on-One Coaching, Status Report (5 min.)

In December, you should have found the time to observe your one-on-one coaches and give them feedback. Discuss issues and concerns.

Discussion of Grade-Level Procedures (20 min.)

Oral Reading Analysis. If you have students who are still struggling with word recognition, begin oral reading analysis with them (Taylor, Harris, Pearson, and Garcia 1995), perhaps on Day 3 or 5, if you have not already done so. In oral reading analysis, you take three, 100-word samples of a student's reading of material not read before at their instructional level (92%–97% accuracy in word recognition). You analyze these samples to determine one problem area to focus on. You provide instruction in this focus area. As a student does subsequent oral readings, you continue to assess in this focus area, monitoring with a progress chart to document the student's growth in the target area. Once a student has made good progress in one problem area, move to another as needed. Oral reading analysis is discussed in greater detail in Chapter 4.

Small-Group Activity. Discuss oral reading analysis as described in Chapter 4. Try oral reading analysis with at least one student over the next month and be prepared to share results at the next month's meeting.

Reciprocal Teaching. Research has shown it takes between fifteen and twenty lessons, spread out over between ten and twenty weeks, for elementary students to learn to use the reciprocal teaching strategy successfully (see Palincsar and Brown 1996). By January, however, if you feel your students are ready, you may have them try the steps of the reciprocal teaching model on their own (see Chapter 4). Discuss with them that this is a way they can study a social studies or science textbook on their own. Have them jot down their questions and summaries for designated chunks of text. You can share these with the group to refine students' ability to ask good questions and to summarize chunks of text.

Small-Group Activity. Discuss with your colleagues whether or not you feel your students are ready to try reciprocal teaching on their own as an independent study strategy. Decide on a plan for trying this with your students sometime before March. If you plan on trying reciprocal teaching as an independent strategy over the next month, jot notes on the lessons, and be prepared to share with your group next month.

Video Sharing (15–30 min.)
Engage in video sharing. Fill out a new video-sharing sheet for February through April (refer back to Figure 7–5).

Preparation for February Meeting (5 min.)
For the February meeting, one or two people per small group should bring in short video clips to share a predetermined piece of an EIR lesson.

February Meeting (60–80 min.)

Status Report on Children's Progress (5–10 min.)

Briefly report on successes you are seeing with your students.

Discuss Grade-Level Procedures and Additional Comprehension Instruction Techniques (15 min.)

▶ By this time, some of you probably have had your students try the steps of the reciprocal teaching model on their own. You need to keep reminding them that this is a way they can study a social studies or science textbook on their own. Again, I would like to recommend that to learn how to do this as an independent strategy, it is probably a good idea for children to jot down their summaries and important questions as well as things that they needed to clarify. With something written down, they have concrete ideas to share with a partner or small group after they are done practicing the RT strategies. However, I wouldn't tell children that they always have to write these steps down. When they are good at the strategies, they may wish to practice them in their heads.

▶ Discuss successes and challenges working with students on using reciprocal teaching strategies on their own as an independent study strategy. Discuss what you did that helped children experience success and feel good about this approach to reciprocal teaching. (It's often seen as less fun than the collaborative group approach.)

▶ Discuss successes and challenges you are experiencing with the cross-age tutoring component. Brainstorm solutions to problems.

▶ If you feel your students are ready for new challenges, you may want to try Transactional Strategies Instruction (TSI) with your students, a more flexible version of Reciprocal Teaching (described in Chapter 4). A set of steps to follow for a series of study group meetings as you learn to use TSI can be found in Figure 7–6.

▶ Or, if you feel your students are ready for new challenges, you may want to turn to narrative texts and use a research-based discussion technique with them on Days 4 and 5 for the remainder of the school year during their EIR lesson time. High level talk about text and discussion techniques are presented in Chapter 4. A set of steps to follow for a series of study group meetings as you learn to use a discussion technique can be found in Figure 7–6.

Group Activity (10 min.)

Those of you who have tried oral reading analysis with students should share your experiences. Help answer one another's questions. When are you doing this? What passages are you using? Discuss challenges. Brainstorm solutions to challenges.

Video Sharing (15–30 min.)

Engage in video sharing.

Preparation for March Meeting (2 min.)

One or two people should bring in short video clips of their EIR lesson to share.

March Meeting (50–75 min.)

Status Report on Children's Progress (5–10 min.)

Briefly report on successes you are seeing with your students. Also discuss any concerns you may have.

Additional Comprehension Techniques (20–25 min.)

Discuss using transactional strategies instruction if you have tried this (see Chapter 4). Alternatively, discuss your recent experiences with high-level talk about text as prompted by one of the discussion techniques described in Chapter 4. Use the framework for study group sessions in Figure 7–6.

Group Activity. Discuss your progress and plans for the rest of the school year for working with your students on an additional comprehension technique. Also, briefly discuss the progress your students are making in word recognition as a result of oral reading analysis.

Video Sharing (15–30 min.)

Engage in video sharing.

Preparation for April Meeting (5 min.)

Before the next meeting, read through the section in Chapter 5 on spring assessments. At the April meeting, you should review spring assessment procedures and answer any questions members of the group may have. One or two people should bring in short video clips of their EIR lesson to share.

April Meeting (50–65 min.)

Status Report on Children's Progress (5–10 min.)

Briefly report on successes you are seeing with your students.

Additional Comprehension Techniques (5–10 min.)

Based on what you chose to study and implement, briefly discuss transactional strategies instruction or high-level talk and writing about text. Be careful of your time so that you have sufficient opportunity to discuss the spring assessments.

Assessments (25–30 min.)

Review the steps for completing the assessments in Chapter 5. Select the passages you will all use from an informal reading inventory. Typically, you should do the assessments during the first two weeks of May before things get hectic with end-of-the-year activities.

Video Sharing (15–30 min.)

Engage in video sharing.

Preparation for May Meeting (2 min.)

Be prepared to discuss your assessments and your overall reflections about the year, as well as your plans for next year.

May Meeting (50–65 min.)

First, I would like to thank you for your hard work implementing the EIR lessons this year and meeting monthly to work through the EIR professional learning sessions. I hope the experience has been a rewarding one for you, and most importantly, for your students. All children deserve the chance to learn to read well, and I commend you on your efforts to help your students make important progress in reading.

Status Report on Children's Progress (5–10 min.)

Share your major successes. How many students were able to stop receiving EIR lessons during the year? How many will require EIR lessons next year?

Discuss Results of Assessment Results (25–35 min.)

Discuss how students did on the assessments and which assessments provided you with the most information. Were there any surprises (e.g., did some students whom you thought would do well not do well? Did some students do much better than you expected?)?

Review Year and Discuss Plans for Next Year (20 min.)

Framework for a Series of Study Group Sessions

1. Decide on the topic you wish to study, based on your students' needs and your needs as teachers. (For example, would EIR students benefit from learning how to use reciprocal teaching as an independent study strategy? Would they benefit from instruction in how to engage in discussions about texts in small groups?)

2. Select a specific research-based technique that you wish to learn, practice, and refine over two or three months. Questions to ask include:
   ▶ Is the technique validated or directly supported by research?
   ▶ Is the technique likely to lead to significant improvements in students' reading ability?
   ▶ Is the technique worth studying for a number of sessions?

3. Choose one or more articles that focus on this particular instructional approach and include detailed information on how to move forward instructionally. Read these articles before the first session.

4. Undertake a series of study sessions each lasting about an hour:
   ▶ *Session 1:*

   Discuss the theory and research behind the technique as well as its implementation in the classroom. (*20 min.*) Decide as a group how members will implement the technique in their classroom before the next session. Perhaps sketch out a tentative lesson plan. (*25 min.*)

   ▶ *Session 2:*

   Discuss what went well and what problems or confusions you experienced as you tried out the technique. Propose solutions to problems and clear up confusions. (*15 min.*)

   Discuss modifications to your teaching. (*20 min.*)

   Decide who will bring a video clip to the next session and who will bring a sample of students' work. (*10 min.*)

   Revisit your action plan. (*10 min.*)

   ▶ *Session 3:*

   Discuss what went well and what problems or confusions you experienced as you tried out the technique. Propose solutions to problems and clear up confusions. (*10 min.*)

   Based on the readings and on teaching experiences, discuss modifications to the technique being studied. (*15 min.*)

   Using the video-sharing protocol (Figure 7–4), watch and discuss the video clip. (*15 min.*) Using the looking-at-student-work protocol (Figure 7–7), examine samples of student work. (*15 min.*)

   Decide who is going to bring a video clip and who is going to bring student work to the next session. (*5 min.*)

   ▶ *Session 4:*

   Discuss what went well and what problems or confusions you experienced. (*10 min.*)

   Propose solutions to problems and clear up confusions. (*10 min.*)

   Based on readings and on teaching experiences, discuss necessary modifications to make next in your teaching. (*10 min.*)

   Using the video-sharing protocol (Figure 7–4), watch and discuss the video clip. (*15 min.*)

   Using the looking-at-student-work-protocol (Figure 7–7), examine samples of student work. (*15 min.*)

   Decide whether to wrap up the study of this technique, schedule additional sessions, or study a new technique. (*10 min.*)

Adapted from Taylor (2010d).

Figure 7–6 Framework for a Series of Study Group Sessions

When teachers look at student work, it is also important that teachers have a protocol to follow. Below is a protocol influenced by the Collaborative Assessment Conference protocol developed by Harvard Project Zero (Blythe, Allen, and Powell 1999. Also see www.lasw.org.).

Protocol for Examining Student Work

1. A facilitator leads the discussion and keeps the group on task.

2. A teacher hands out a few pieces of student work related to the study group topic from a cross section of students (e.g., three unidentified pieces, one from a higher-ability student, one from an average-ability student, and one from a lower-ability student). The teacher explains the assignment and asks a focusing question. (*2 min.*)

3. The presenting teacher answers any clarifying questions posed by group members. (*1–2 min.*)

4. The group examines and describes the work. What skills/strengths are evident? What don't the students know or what aren't the students able to do? What features of the work stand out, what surprised you? (*5–7 min.*)

5. Several areas or skills in need of improvement are identified, and the group shares research-based ideas to improve instruction. The facilitator may remind the group of the original focusing question of the presenting teacher. (*5–7 min.*)

6. The presenting teacher reflects on what she will try to do to improve instruction by responding to the members' comments or questions. Other members decide on something they learned from the process that they will implement to improve their instruction as well. (*2 min.*)

© 2011 by Barbara M. Taylor from *Catching Readers, Grades 4/5*. Portsmouth, NH: Heinemann.

Figure 7–7 Protocol for Examining Student Work

Training One-on-One Coaches

The one-on-one coaching component of EIR for students who need more support in word recognition is a very important piece, but one that sometimes gets overlooked simply because it can be difficult to put in place if people are not readily available to read with students every day. However, the students who are having difficulties with word recognition make much better progress in reading if they have a chance every day, or as close to every day as possible, to practice reading their newest EIR story with a person who has been trained in how to coach, not tell them words, as they get stuck. Also, in this one-on-one situation, children get to demonstrate to themselves their decoding abilities and don't have the pressure of another child sitting next to them calling out a word before they do.

Ceilia Huxley, an EIR trainer, developed the material in this section to train coaches. She has used it successfully with instructional aides and parent volunteers.

Coaching Training in One-on-One Coaching

Follow the agenda in Figure 7–8 to provide training to volunteers, educational assistants, and older students who will be coaching EIR students as they read their EIR stories in a one-on-one situation. To introduce EIR, first review the basic elements of the program (Figure 7–9).

Next, describe coaching. Have participants read over Figure 7–9. Explain that coaching is giving children prompts, encouraging them, and praising them as they attempt to figure out words on their own. Students have been learning a number of different strategies to figure out unknown words as they come to them. The purpose of coaching is to help children to learn to depend on themselves so they become good, independent readers. Show Figure 7–11 for prompts the coaches can use as they are working with the children.

To illustrate coaching show the following video clip:

- **Grade 4/5, Video 1** Teacher working with a group of grade 4 children

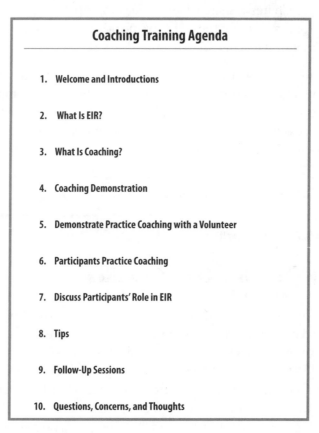

Coaching Training Agenda

1. Welcome and Introductions

2. What Is EIR?

3. What Is Coaching?

4. Coaching Demonstration

5. Demonstrate Practice Coaching with a Volunteer

6. Participants Practice Coaching

7. Discuss Participants' Role in EIR

8. Tips

9. Follow-Up Sessions

10. Questions, Concerns, and Thoughts

Figure 7–8 Coaching Training Agenda

Basic Elements of EIR

▸ Twenty minutes of daily supplemental reading instruction to a small group of six or seven struggling readers.

▸ Children receiving EIR participate in all of the regular reading instruction.

▸ Five-day cycle of reading and rereading informational books. Focus on attacking multisyllabic words, developing fluency, discussing vocabulary at point of contact in the text, practicing comprehension strategies, and engaging in high-level talk and writing about text.

▸ Teacher concentrates on coaching students in their use of reading strategies.

▸ Preparation for (a) reading the grade 4 or 5 EIR books to second or third graders who need extra support in reading and (b) coaching these younger students as they read stories introduced in their own EIR lessons. (If cross-age tutoring is omitted, students work one day a week with an EIR partner instead.)

▸ Transfer of EIR reading strategies to grade-level texts.

▸ Parent involvement.

Figure 7–9 Basic Elements of EIR

Independent Coaching Role

▸ Work with one child at a time.

▸ Classroom teacher gives you the book to use.

▸ Child has a copy of the book.

▸ Assist child in reading the book.

▸ Reinforce strategies.

▸ Give appropriate praise.

Figure 7–10 Independent Coaching Role

Prompts for Teaching Children Decoding and Self-Monitoring Strategies for Multisyllabic Words

▸ Can you reread that? Did that make sense?

▸ You did a great job of figuring out that word. How did you do it?

▸ I like the way you self-corrected. How did you do that?

▸ Let's look at that word again. You said _____. Does that make sense (or look and sound right)?

Steps for Decoding Multisyllabic Words

▸ Break the word into chunks (approximate syllables) with one vowel (or vowel team) per chunk.

▸ Be flexible as you sound out the chunks, especially with the vowel sounds. If one sound doesn't work, try another.

▸ Remember to use context clues.

▸ After you sound out the chunks, try it again only faster.

▸ Remember that this will only get you close to the right word. Keep thinking of context.

Figure 7–11 Prompts for Teaching Children Decoding and Self-Monitoring Strategies for Multisyllabic Words

Tips for Working with Children

▸ Let the child do the work. Do as little as possible for him or her.

▸ Have your strategy sheet with you. Use the strategies consistently to foster independence. (Figure 7–11)

▸ Have the child reread from the beginning of the sentence once, pausing to work on a word.

▸ Praise the child for successful use of strategies.

▸ When a child uses a strategy correctly, use the phrase "That's what good readers do!"

▸ When a child is struggling, refocus their attention. Say, "Take another look at that word," or, "Try again."

Figure 7–12 Tips for Working with Children

Conduct a coaching demonstration by modeling, with a volunteer, and through partner practice. Model coaching by working through a story. Then, ask for a volunteer who will read another text as you coach. Finally, let people practice coaching with a partner by using a third text.

In conclusion, return to Figure 7–10 and Figure 7–11 to review the coach's role. Also look at Figure 7–12, which provides tips for working with children. Ask for questions, thoughts, concerns. Schedule another session once the coaches have been working with children for 4 or 5 weeks.

Summary

I cannot stress enough the importance of the ongoing professional learning experiences. While many believe this component is an extra, I have found that teachers who engage in professional learning experiences with colleagues feel especially successful and, in turn, their students are successful readers.

It is my hope that this book, the companion books for other grades (Taylor 2010a; 2010b; 2010c; forthcoming), and my book on school-based reading improvement (Taylor 2011) will help you and your school teach students to read well. It is also my hope that this book has provided you with the information you need to implement EIR, either as an individual classroom teacher trying to improve your practice, or as part of a school improvement initiative. Should you have additional questions, go to the Heinemann Web site at www.heinemann.com/taylor for additional resources on EIR and search by Taylor or *Catching Readers*, or go to www.earlyinterventioninreading.com.

Finally, it is my hope that you are able to invest the time needed to learn about and implement EIR in your classroom, because when you do, you will feel tremendous pride in what your students will accomplish, especially knowing you were instrumental in showing them the way. Thank you for the important work you do with and for children.

Works Cited

Adams, M. J. 1990. *Beginning to Read: Thinking and Learning About Print.* Cambridge, MA: MIT Press.

Allington, R. L., and P. H. Johnston. 2002. *Reading to Learn: Lessons from Exemplary Fourth-Grade Classrooms.* New York: Guilford.

Au, K. H. 2006. *Multicultural Issues and Literacy Achievement.* Mahwah, NJ: Lawrence Erlbaum.

Barrett, J. 1988. *Animals Should Definitely Not Wear Clothing.* New York: Aladdin.

Baumann, J. F., and E. J. Kame'enui. 2004. *Vocabulary Instruction: Research to Practice.* New York: Guilford.

Bear, D. R., M. Invernizzi, S. Templeton, and F. Johnston. 2007. *Words Their Way: Word Study for Phonics, Vocabulary, and Spelling Instruction.* 4th ed. Upper Saddle River, NJ: Pearson/Merrill Prentice Hall.

Beck, I. L. 2006. *Making Sense of Phonics: The Hows and Whys.* New York: Guilford.

Beck, I. L., and M. G. McKeown. 2006. *Improving Comprehension with Questioning the Author: A Fresh and Expanded View of a Powerful Approach.* New York: Scholastic.

Beck, I. L., M. G. McKeown, and L. Kucan. 2002. *Bringing Words to Life: Robust Vocabulary Instruction.* New York: Guilford.

Beck, I. L., M. G. McKeown, C. Sandora, L. Kucan, and J. Worthy. 1996. "Questioning the Author: A Yearlong Classroom Implementation to Engage Students with Text." *The Elementary School Journal* 96 (4): 385–414.

Bergman, J. L. 1992. "SAIL—A Way to Success and Independence for Low-Achieving Readers." *The Reading Teacher* 45 (8): 598–602.

Barry, Sharon L. 2005, February. "Do Animals Have Feelings?" *Ranger Rick* 39 (2): 2–10.

Blachowicz, C., and P. Fisher. 2000. "Vocabulary Instruction." In *Handbook of Reading Research, Volume III,* ed. M. L. Kamil, P. B. Mosenthal, P. D. Pearson, and R. Barr. Mahwah, NJ: Lawrence Erlbaum.

———. 2002. *Teaching Vocabulary in All Classrooms.* 2d ed. Upper Saddle River, NJ: Pearson/Merrill Prentice Hall.

Bohn, C. M., A. D. Roehrig, and M. Pressley. 2004. "The First Days of School in the Classrooms of Two More Effective and Four Less Effective Primary-Grades Teachers." *The Elementary School Journal* 104: 271–87.

Brown, R., P. B. El-Dinary, M. Pressley, and L. Coy-Ogan. 1995. "A Transactional Strategies Approach to Reading Instruction." *The Reading Teacher* 49 (3): 256–57.

Chorzempa, B. F., and S. Graham. 2006. "Primary-Grade Teachers' Use of Within-Class Ability Grouping in Reading." *Journal of Educational Psychology* 98: 529–41.

Christensen, C. A., and J. A. Bowey. 2005. "The Efficacy of Orthographic Rime, Grapheme-Phoneme Correspondence, and Implicit Phonics Approaches to Teaching Decoding Skills." *Scientific Studies of Reading* 9: 327–49.

Clay, M. 1993. *Reading Recovery: A Guidebook for Teachers in Training.* Portsmouth, NH: Heinemann.

Connor, C. M., F. J. Morrison, and L. E. Katch. 2004. "Beyond the Reading Wars: Exploring the Effect of Child-Instruction Interactions on Growth in Early Reading." *Scientific Studies of Reading* 8: 305–36.

Consortium for Responsible School Change. 2005. *Description of Common Findings Across Multiple Studies on School Change in Reading.* University of Minnesota, Minnesota Center for Reading Research.

Cunningham, P. M. 2009. *Phonics They Use: Words for Reading and Writing.* 5th ed. Boston: Pearson.

Cunningham, P. M., and D. R. Smith. 2008. *Beyond Retelling: Toward Higher Level Thinking and Big Ideas.* Newark, DE: International Reading Association.

Day, J. P., D. L. Spiegel, J. McLellan, and V. B. Brown. 2002. *Moving Forward with Literature Circles.* New York: Scholastic.

Dolezal, S. E., L. M. Welsh, M. Pressley, and M. M. Vincent. 2003. "How Nine Third-Grade Teachers Motivate Student Academic Engagement." *Elementary School Journal* 103: 239–67.

Duke, N. K., and V. S. Bennett-Armistead. 2003. *Reading and Writing Informational Text in the Primary Grades: Research-Based Practices.* New York: Scholastic.

Edwards, P. A. 2004. *Children's Literacy Development: Making It Happen Through School, Family, and Community Involvement.* Boston: Pearson/Allyn & Bacon.

Fleischman, S. 1994. *The Scarebird.* New York: Greenwillow.

Foorman, B. R., and J. Torgesen. 2001. "Critical Elements of Classroom and Small-Group Instruction Promote Reading Success in All Children." *Learning Disabilities Research and Practice* 16: 203–12.

Foorman, B. R., C. Schatsneider, M. N. Eakin, J. M. Fletcher, L. C. Moats, and D. J. Francis. 2006. "The Impact of Instructional Practices in Grades 1 and 2 on Reading and Spelling Achievement in High Poverty Schools." *Contemporary Educational Psychology* 31: 1–29.

Fountas, I., and G. S. Pinnell. 2001. *Guided Reading and Writing: Grades 3–6*. Portsmouth, NH: Heinemann.

Fuchs, L. S., D. Fuchs, M. K. Hosp, and J. R. Jenkins. 2001. "Oral Reading Fluency as an Indicator of Reading Competence: A Theoretical, Empirical, and Historical Analysis." *Scientific Studies of Reading* 5: 239–56.

Gaetz, T. 1991. "The Effects of a Self-Monitoring Checklist on Elementary Students' Post-Reading Question-Answering Performance." Unpublished doctoral dissertation, University of Minnesota.

Galda, L., B. Cullinan, and L. Sipe. 2010. *Literature and the Child*. 7th ed. Belmont, CA: Thomson/Wadsworth.

Gaskins, I. W. 2005. *Success with Struggling Readers: The Benchmark School Approach.* New York: Guilford.

Goldenberg, C. 1992. "Instructional Conversations: Promoting Comprehension Through Discussion." *The Reading Teacher* 46: 316–26.

Graves, M. F. 2007. "Conceptual and Empirical Bases for Providing Struggling Readers with Multifaceted and Long-Term Vocabulary Instruction." In *Effective Instruction for Struggling Readers K–6*, ed. B. M. Taylor and J. E. Ysseldyke, 55–83. New York: Teachers College Press.

Guthrie, J. T., A. Wigfield, and C. VonSecker. 2000. "Effects of Integrated Instruction on Motivation and Strategy Use in Reading." *Journal of Educational Psychology* 92: 331–41.

Guthrie, J. T., A. Wigfield, P. Barbosa, K. C. Perencevich, A. Taboada, M. H. Davis, et al. 2004. "Increasing Reading Comprehension and Engagement Through Concept-Oriented Reading Instruction." *Journal of Educational Psychology* 96: 403–23.

Guzetti, B., ed. 2002. *Literacy in America: An Encyclopedia of History, Theory, and Practice.* Santa Barbara, CA: ABE-CLIO.

Hamre, B. K., and R. C. Pianta. 2005. "Can Instructional and Emotional Support in the First-Grade Classroom Make a Difference for Children at Risk of School Failure?" *Child Development* 76(5): 949–67.

Hasbrouck, J., and G. A. Tindal. 2006. "Oral Reading Fluency Norms: A Valuable Assessment Tool for Reading Teachers." *The Reading Teacher* 59 (7): 636–44.

Heffernan, L. 2004. *Critical Literacy and Writer's Workshop.* Newark, DE: International Reading Association.

Hiebert, E. H., and B. M. Taylor. 2000. "Beginning Reading Instruction: Research on Early Interventions." In *Handbook of Reading Research, Volume III*, ed. M. L. Kamil, P. B. Mosenthal, P. D. Pearson, and R. Barr. Mahwah, NJ: Lawrence Erlbaum.

Hiebert, E. H., J. M. Colt, S. L. Catto, and E. C. Gury. 1992. "Reading and Writing of First-Grade Students in a Restructured Chapter I Program." *American Educational Research Journal* 29: 545–72.

Johns, J. L., and R. L. Berglund. 2005. *Fluency Strategies and Assessments.* Dubuque, IA: Kendall-Hunt.

Johnson, D. 2008. *Teaching Literacy in Fourth Grade.* New York: Guilford.

Juel, C., and C. Minden-Cupp. 2000. "Learning to Read Words: Linguistic Units and Instructional Strategies." *Reading Research Quarterly* 35: 458–92.

Kelley, M. J., and N. Clausen-Grace. 2007. *Comprehension Shouldn't Be Silent.* Newark, DE: International Reading Association.

Kletsien, S. B., and M. J. Dreher. 2005. *Informational Text in K–3 Classrooms: Helping Children Read and Write.* Newark, DE: International Reading Association.

Klingner, J. K., S. Vaughn, M. E. Arguelles, M. T. Hughes, and S. A. Leftwich. 2004. "Collaborative Strategic Reading: Real World Lessons from Classroom Teachers." *Remedial and Special Education* 25: 291–302.

Knapp, M. S. 1995. *Teaching for Meaning in High-Poverty Classrooms.* New York: Teachers College Press.

Kuhn, M. R., and S. A. Stahl. 2003. "Fluency: A Review of Developmental and Remedial Practices." *Journal of Educational Psychology* 95: 3–21.

Lapp, D., D. Fisher, and T. D. Wolsey. 2009. *Literacy Growth for Every Child: Differentiated Small-Group Instruction, K–6.* New York: Guilford.

Leslie, L., and J. Caldwell. 2006. *Qualitative Reading Inventory 4.* Boston: Pearson.

Lipson. M. Y. 2007. *Teaching Reading Beyond the Primary Grades.* New York: Scholastic.

Lipson, M. L., J. H. Mosenthal, J. Mekkelsen, and B. Russ. 2004. "Building Knowledge and Fashioning Success One School at a Time." *The Reading Teacher* 57(6): 534–42.

Lobel, A. 1981. *Fables.* New York: HarperCollins.

Manning, M., G. Morrison, and D. Camp. 2009. *Creating the Best Literacy Block Ever.* New York: Scholastic.

Mathes, P. G., C. A. Denton, J. M. Fletcher, J. L. Anthony, D. J. Francis, and C. Schatschneider. 2005. "The Effects of Theoretically Different Instruction and Student Characteristics on the Skills of Struggling Readers." *Reading Research Quarterly* 40: 148–82.

McCormick, R. L., and J. Paratore. 2005. *After Early Intervention, Then What: Teaching Struggling Readers in Grades Three and Beyond.* Newark, DE: International Reading Association.

McKee, J., and D. Ogle. 2005. *Integrating Instruction: Literacy and Science.* New York: Guilford.

McKeown, M. G., I. L. Beck, and R. G. K. Blake. 2009. "Rethinking Reading Comprehension Instruction: A Comparison of Instruction for Strategies and Content Approaches." *Reading Research Quarterly* 44 (3): 218–53.

McMahon, S. I., and J. Wells. 2007. *Teaching Literacy in Fifth Grade.* New York: Guilford.

National Reading Panel. 2000. *Teaching Children to Read: An Evidence-Based Assessment of the Scientific Research Literature on Reading and Its Implications for Reading Instruction.* Rockville, MD: National Institute for Child Health and Human Development, National Institutes of Health.

Oczkus, L. D. 2003. *Reciprocal Teaching at Work: Strategies for Improving Reading Comprehension.* Newark, DE: International Reading Association.

Olness, R. 2007. *Using Literature to Enhance Content Area Instruction: A Guide for K–5 Teachers.* Newark, DE: International Reading Association.

Palincsar, A., and A. Brown. 1986. "Interactive Teaching to Promote Independent Learning from Text." *The Reading Teacher* 39 (8): 771–77.

———. 1984. "Reciprocal Teaching of Comprehension-Fostering and Comprehension-Monitoring Activities." *Cognition and Instruction* 2: 117–75.

Paratore, J. R., and R. L. McCormack, eds. 2007. *Classroom Literacy Assessment: Making Sense of What Students Know and Do.* New York: Guilford.

Pikulski, J. 1994. "Preventing Reading Failure: A Review of Five Effective Programs." *The Reading Teacher* 48: 30–39.

Pinkwater, D. 1993. *The Big Orange Splot.* New York: Scholastic.

Pinnell, G., M. Fried, and R. Estice. 1990. "Reading Recovery: Learning How to Make a Difference." *The Reading Teacher* 90: 160–83.

Pressley, M. 2001. *Effective Beginning Reading Instruction: Executive Summary and Paper Commissioned by the National Reading Conference.* Chicago, IL: National Reading Conference.

———. 2006. *Reading Instruction That Works: The Case for Balanced Teaching.* 3d ed. New York: Guilford.

Pressley, M., P. B. El-Dinary, I. Gaskins, T. Schuder, J. L. Bergman, J. Almasi, and R. Brown. 1992. "Beyond Direct Explanation: Transactional Instruction of Reading Comprehension Strategies." *Elementary School Journal* 92: 511–54.

Pressley, M., S. E. Dolezal, L. M. Raphael, L. Mohan, A. D. Roehrig, and K. Bogner. 2003. *Motivating Primary-Grade Students.* New York: Guilford.

Pressley, M., L. Mohan, L. M. Raphael, and L. Fingeret. 2007. "How Does Bennett Woods Elementary School Produce Such High Reading and Writing Achievement?" *Journal of Educational Psychology* 99 (2): 221–40.

Pressley, M., R. Wharton-McDonald, J. Mistretta-Hampston, and M. Echevarria. 1998. "Literacy Instruction in 10 Fourth- and Fifth-Grade Classrooms in Upstate New York." *Scientific Studies of Reading* 2: 159–94.

Raphael, T. E., and S. I. McMahon. 1994. "Book Club: An Alternative Framework for Reading Instruction." *The Reading Teacher* 48 (2): 102–16.

Raphael, T. E, L. S. Pardo, and K. Highfield. 2002. *Book Club: A Literature-Based Curriculum.* 2d ed. Lawrence, MA: Small Planet.

Raphael, T. E., K. Highfield, and K. H. Au. 2006. *QAR Now.* New York: Scholastic.

Rasinski, T. V. 2003. *The Fluent Reader: Oral Reading Strategies for Building Word Recognition, Fluency, and Comprehension.* New York: Scholastic.

Rosenshine, B., and C. Meister. 1994. "Reciprocal Teaching: A Review of the Research." *Review of Educational Research* 64(4): 479–530.

Routman, R. 2008. *Teaching Essentials.* Portsmouth, NH: Heinemann.

Saunders, W. M., and C. Goldenberg. 1999. "Effects of Instructional Conversations and Literature Logs on Limited and Fluent English Proficient Students' Story Comprehension and Thematic Understanding." *The Elementary School Journal* 99: 279–301.

Seravallo, J. 2010. *Reading Instruction in Small Groups.* Portsmouth, NH: Heinemann.

Slavin, R. E., A. Cheung, C. Groff, and C. Lake. 2008. "Effective Reading Programs for Middle and High School: A Best Evidence Synthesis." *Reading Research Quarterly* 43 (3): 290–322.

Slavin, R. E., C. Lake, B. Chambers, A. Cheung, and S. Davis. 2009. "Effective Reading Programs for the Elementary Grades: A Best-Evidence Synthesis." *Review of Educational Research* 79: 1391–1466.

Snow, C. E., M. S. Burns, and P. Griffin, eds. 1998. *Preventing Reading Difficulties in Young Children.* Washington, DC: National Academy.

Southall, M. 2009. *Differentiated Small-Group Reading Lessons.* New York: Scholastic.

Stahl, K. A., G. E. Garcia, E. B. Bauer, P. D. Pearson, and B. M. Taylor. 2006. "Making the Invisible Visible: The Development of a Comprehension Assessment System." In *Reading Research at Work: Foundations of Effective Practice,* ed. K. A. Stahl and M. C. McKenna, 425–36. New York: Guilford.

Stahl, S. A. 2001. "Teaching Phonics and Phonemic Awareness." In *Handbook of Early Literacy Research,* ed. S. B. Neuman and D. Dickenson. New York: Guilford.

Swan, E. A. *Concept-Oriented Reading Instruction: Engaging Classrooms, Lifelong Learners.*

Taberski, S. 2000. *On Solid Ground: Strategies for Teaching Reading K–3.* Portsmouth, NH: Heinemann.

Taylor, B. M. 2001. *The Early Intervention in Reading Program: Research and Development Spanning Twelve Years.* www.earlyinterventioninreading.com.

———. 2010a. *Catching Readers, Grade 1*. Portsmouth, NH: Heinemann.

———. 2010b. *Catching Readers, Grade 2*. Portsmouth, NH: Heinemann.

———. 2010c. *Catching Readers, Grade 3*. Portsmouth, NH: Heinemann.

———. 2011. *Catching Schools: An Action Guide to School-Wide Reading Improvement*. Portsmouth, NH: Heinemann.

Taylor, B., and B. Frye. 1992. "Comprehension Strategy Instruction in the Intermediate Grades." *Reading Research and Instruction* 32: 39–49.

Taylor, B., B. Frye, and G. Maruyama. 1990. "Time Spent Reading and Reading Growth." *American Educational Research Journal* 27: 351–62.

Taylor, B. M., G. E. Garcia, and P. D. Pearson. 2007. "Comprehension Strategies, High Level Talk About Text, and Vocabulary: Effective Comprehension Instruction in Grades 2–5." Invited paper presented at the Research Conference, International Reading Association, Toronto, Canada.

Taylor, B. M., B. Hanson, K. J. Justice-Swanson, and S. Watts. 1997. "Helping Struggling Readers: Linking Small Group Intervention with Cross-Age Tutoring." *The Reading Teacher* 51: 196–209.

Taylor, B. M., L. Harris, P. D. Pearson, and G. E. Garcia. 1995. *Reading Difficulties: Instruction and Assessment*. 2d ed. New York: Random House.

Taylor, B. M., P. D. Pearson, K. Clark, and S. Walpole. 2000. "Effective Schools and Accomplished Teachers: Lessons About Primary Grade Reading Instruction in Low-Income Schools." *Elementary School Journal* 101 (2): 121–66.

Taylor, B. M., P. D. Pearson, D. S. Peterson, and M. C. Rodriguez. 2003. "Reading Growth in High-Poverty Classrooms: The Influence of Teacher Practices That Encourage Cognitive Engagement in Literacy Learning." *Elementary School Journal* 104: 3–28.

———. 2005. "The CIERA School Change Framework: An Evidence-Based Approach to Professional Development and School Reading Improvement." *Reading Research Quarterly* 40 (1): 40–69.

Taylor, B. M., D. S. Peterson, M. Marx, and M. Chein. 2007. "Scaling Up a Reading Reform in High-Poverty Elementary Schools." In *Effective Instruction for Struggling Readers, K–6*, ed. B. M. Taylor and J. E. Ysseldyke. New York: Teachers College Press.

Taylor, B. M., D. S. Peterson, P. D. Pearson, and M. C. Rodriguez. 2002. "Looking Inside Classrooms: Reflecting on the 'How' as Well as the 'What' in Effective Reading Instruction." *The Reading Teacher* 56: 70–79.

Taylor, B. M., M. Pressley, and P. D. Pearson. 2002. "Research-Supported Characteristics of Teachers and Schools That Promote Reading Achievement." In *Teaching Reading: Effective Schools, Accomplished Teachers*, ed. B. M. Taylor and P. D. Pearson. Mahwah, NJ: Lawrence Erlbaum.

Taylor, B. M., T. E. Raphael, and K. H. Au. 2010. "Reading and School Reform." In *Handbook of Reading Research, Volume 4*, ed. M. Kamil, P. D. Pearson, P. Afflerbach, and E. Moje. New York: Routledge.

Taylor, B. M., R. Short, B. Frye, and B. Shearer. 1992. "Classroom Teachers Prevent Reading Failure Among Low-Achieving First-Grade Students." *The Reading Teacher* 45: 592–97.

Valli, L., R. G. Croninger, and K. Walters. 2007. "Who (Else) Is the Teacher? Cautionary Notes on Teacher Accountability Systems." *American Journal of Education* 113: 635–62.

Van den Branden, K. 2000. "Does Negotiation of Meaning Promote Reading Comprehension? A Study of Multilingual Primary School Classes." *Reading Research Quarterly* 35: 426–43.

Wilkinson, I. A. G. 2009. "Discussion Methods." In *Psychology of Classroom Learning: An Encyclopedia,* ed. E. M. Anderman and L. H. Anderman. Detroit, MI: Gale/Cengage.

Recommended Professional Readings

Resources on Phonics and Word Recognition Instruction

Bear, D. R., M. Invernizzi, S. Templeton, and F. Johnston. 2007. *Words Their Way: Word Study for Phonics, Vocabulary, and Spelling Instruction*, 4th edition. Upper Saddle River, NJ: Pearson/Merrill Prentice Hall.

Beck, I. 2006. *Making Sense of Phonics: The Hows and Whys.* New York: Guilford.

Cunningham, P. 2009. *Phonics They Use: Words for Reading and Writing*, 5th edition. Boston: Pearson.

Gaskins, I. W., L. C. Ehri, C. Cress, C. O'Hara, and D. Donnelly. 1996. "Procedures for Word Learning: Making Discoveries About Words." *The Reading Teacher* 50: 312–27.

Resources on Fluency

Johns, J. L. and R. L. Berglund. 2005. *Fluency Strategies and Assessments.* Dubuque, IA: Kendall-Hunt.

Rasinski, T. V. 2003. *The Fluent Reader: Oral Reading Strategies for Building Word Recognition, Fluency, and Comprehension.* New York: Scholastic.

Samuels, S. J., and A. Farstrup (eds.). 2006. *What Research Has to Say About Fluency Instruction*, 3rd edition. Newark, DE: International Reading Association.

Stahl, S. A. and M. R. Kuhn. 2002. "Making It Sound Like Language: Developing Fluency." *The Reading Teacher* 55(6), 582–84.

Resources on Vocabulary

Bauman, J. F., and E. J. Kamen'eui (eds.). 2004. *Vocabulary Instruction: Research to Practice.* New York: Guilford Press.

Beck, I., M. McKeown, and L. Kucan. 2002. *Bringing Words to Life: Robust Vocabulary Instruction.* New York: Guilford.

Blachowicz, C., and P. Fisher. 2002. *Teaching Vocabulary in All Classrooms*, second edition. Upper Saddle River, NJ: Pearson/Merrill Prentice Hall.

Graves, M. F. 2007. "Conceptual and Empirical Bases for Providing Struggling Readers with Multifaceted and Long-Term Vocabulary Instruction." In B. M.

Taylor and J. E. Ysseldyke (eds.), *Effective Instruction for Struggling Readers K–6* (55–83). New York: Teachers College Press.

Resources on Comprehension Strategies

Block, C., and M. Pressley (eds.). 2002. *Comprehension Strategies: Research-based Practices.* New York: Guilford.

Kelley, M. J., and N. Clausen-Grace. 2007. *Comprehension Shouldn't Be Silent.* Newark, DE: International Reading Association.

Klingner, J. K., S. Vaughn, M. E. Arguelles, M. T. Hughes, and S. A. Leftwich. 2004. "Collaborative Strategic Reading: Real World Lessons from Classroom Teachers." *Remedial and Special Education* 25, 291–302.

Moss, B., and D. Lapp. 2010. *Teaching New Literacies in Grades 4–6.* New York: Guilford.

Raphael, T. E., K. Highfield, and K. H. Au. 2006. *QAR Now.* New York: Scholastic.

Resources on Comprehension: High Level Talk and Writing about Text

Cunningham, P. M., and D. R. Smith. 2008. *Beyond Retelling: Toward Higher Level Thinking and Big Ideas.* Newark, DE: International Reading Association.

Day, J. P., D. L. Spiegel, J. McLellan, and V. B. Brown. 2002. *Moving Forward with Literature Circles.* New York: Scholastic

Galda, L., B. Cullinan, and L. Sipe. 2010. *Literature and the Child,* 7th edition. Belmont, CA: Thomson/Wadsworth.

Kelley, M. J., and N. Clausen-Grace. 2007. *Comprehension Shouldn't Be Silent.* Newark, DE: International Reading Association.

Olness, R. 2007. *Using Literature to Enhance Content Area Instruction: A Guide for K–5 Teachers.* Newark, DE: International Reading Association.

Raphael, T. E., L. S. Pardo, and L. Highfield. 2002. *Book Club: A Literature-based Curriculum.* Second edition. Lawrence, MA: Small Planet.

Raphael, T. R., and S. McMahon. 1994. "Book Club: An Alternative Framework for Reading Instruction." *The Reading Teacher* 48(2), 102–16.

Resources on Balanced, Differentiated, or Integrated Instruction

Fountas, I. C., and G. S. Pinnell. 2001. *Guiding Readers and Writers, Grades 3–6.* Portsmouth, NH: Heinemann.

Lapp, D., D. Fisher, and T. D. Wolsey. 2009. *Literacy Growth for Every Child: Differentiated Small-Group Instruction, K–6.* New York: Guilford.

McKee, J., and D. Ogle. 2005. *Integrating Instruction: Literacy and Science.* New York: Guilford.

Pressley, M. 2006. *Reading Instruction That Works: The Case for Balanced Teaching,* 3rd edition. New York: Guilford.

Routman, R. 2008. *Teaching Essentials: Expecting the Most and Getting the Best from Every Learner, K–8.* Portsmouth, NH: Heinemann.

Routman, R. 2003. *Reading Essentials: The Specifics You Need to Teach Reading Well.* Portsmouth, NH: Heinemann.

Resources on Support for Struggling Readers

Fuchs, D., L. Fuchs, and S. Vaughn (eds.). 2008. *Response to Intervention: An Overview for Educators.* Newark, DE: International Reading Association.

Gaskins, I. W. 2004. *Success with Struggling Readers: The Benchmark School Approach.* New York: Guilford.

McCormick, S. 2007. *Instructing Students Who Have Literacy Problems,* 5th edition. Upper Saddle River, NJ: Pearson.

Taylor, B. M. 2010b. *Catching Readers, Grade 3.* Portsmouth, NH: Heinemann.

Tyner, B., and S. E. Green. 2005. *Small-Group Reading Instruction: A Differentiated Teaching Model for Intermediate Grade Readers, Grades 3–8.* Newark, DE: International Reading Association.

Vaughn, S., J. Wanzek, and J. M. Fletcher. 2007. "Multiple Tiers of Intervention: A Framework for Prevention and Identification of Students with Reading/ Learning Disabilities." In B. M. Taylor and J. E. Ysseldyke (eds.), *Effective Instruction for Struggling Readers, K–6* (173–95). New York: Teachers College Press.

Resources on Motivating, Effective Pedagogy

Allington, R. L. and P H. Johnston. 2002. *Reading to Learn: Lessons from Exemplary Fourth-Grade Classrooms.* New York: Guilford.

Connor, C. M., F. J. Morrison, and L. E. Katch. 2004. "Beyond the Reading Wars: Exploring the Effect of Child-Instruction Interactions on Growth in Early Reading." *Scientific Studies of Reading* 8, 305–36.

Kelley, M. J., and N. Clausen-Grace. 2007. *Comprehension Shouldn't Be Silent.* Newark, DE: International Reading Association.

Olness, R. 2007. *Using Literature to Enhance Content-Area Instruction: A Guide for K–5 Teachers.* Newark, DE: International Reading Association.

Pressley, M. 2006. *Reading Instruction That Works: The Case for Balanced Teaching,* 3rd edition. New York: Guilford.

Pressley, M., S. E. Dolezal, L. M. Raphael, L. Mohan, A. D. Roehrig, and K. Bogner. 2003. *Motivating Primary-Grade Students.* New York: Guilford.

Resources on Assessments

McKenna, M., and S. Stahl. 2003. *Assessment for Reading Instruction.* New York: Guilford.

Paratore, J. R., and R. L. McCormick, (eds.) 2007. *Classroom Reading Assessment: Making Sense of What Students Know and Do.* New York: Guilford.

Pressley, M. 2006. *Reading Instruction That Works: The Case for Balanced Teaching,* 3rd edition. New York: Guilford.

Resources on Culturally Responsive Instruction

Au, K. 2006. *Multicultural Issues and Literacy Achievement.* Mahwah, NJ: Lawrence Erlbaum.

Gaitan, C. D. 2006. *Building Culturally Responsive Classrooms: A Guide for K–6 Teachers.* Thousand Oaks, CA: Corwin.

For a list and review of books for teachers on English language learners, see Opitz, M. F., and J. L. Harding-DeKam. 2007. "Teaching English-Language Learners." *The Reading Teacher* 60(6): 590–93.

Resources on School-Wide Reading Programs and Effective Schools

Allington, R. L., and S. A. Walmsley (eds.). 2007. *No Quick Fix: Rethinking Literacy Programs in American's Elementary Schools* (RTI ed.). New York: Teachers College Press.

Resnick, L. B., and S. Hampton. 2009. *"Reading and Writing Grade by Grade, Revised Edition.* Newark, DE: International Reading Association and NCEE.

Taylor, B. M. 2011. *Catching Schools: An Action Guide to School-Wide Reading Improvement.* Portsmouth, NH: Heinemann.

Taylor, B. M., and P. D. Pearson (eds.). 2002. *Teaching Reading: Effective Schools/ Accomplished Teachers.* Mahwah, NJ: Lawrence Erlbaum.